Straight
From My
Heart

Bob Sluys

. . . no, I didn't bribe them . . .

"Its a story of perseverance, always bouncing back . . ."
                                                    —Devorah

"You took a very serious subject, shed answers and light into it and added humor. Honestly, great job . . ."   —Jeff

"I really enjoyed it as it was deadly serious but managed to leave us with a good feeling and as though you didn't let it all embitter you for more than three minutes . . . I'm going to go to the kitchen and cry over some tea. Thanks for sharing, as they say . . ."   —Jenny

"Narcissistic and self-absorbed—yet highly entertaining and 98% accurate. . ."   —Dr. Block

"The best thing you've ever done—not a crusade, but interesting"
                                                    —John

"Very funny, humorous take on some serious, worrisome and painful stuff.   —Dean

I was truly honored to read your story. I loved it . . . This certainly is a eye opener about how horrible and painful open heart surgery is. I mean, we all know it's bad, but your description takes it to a whole new level . . . I would be writing a book too if I had survived that . . . Wow! I really do love reading your writing. Even with talking about going thru pure hell, to put it lightly, you can still make it entertaining to read about, while still getting across the seriousness of the situation.   —Jen

"It's over? I want more!   —Pat

" . . . when reading your story my emotions ran from joy to relief, to sadness to awe . . ."   —Kathie

". . . you put it out there in honesty and truthfulness with all the pain, suffering humor and insight that gives this writing substance."
                                                    —Dave

"Riveting—I don't know what to say . . ."   —Joey

This Edition -   ISBN: 978-0-9890875-1-3
Soft Cover Full Color Edition -   ISBN: 978-0-9890875-0-6
Hard Cover Edition -   ISBN: 978-0-9890875-2-0

Visit Straight From My Heart on facebook at:
http://www.facebook.com/pages/Straight-From-My-Heart/
170416243101870?ref=hl

Cover art *"GET WELL CARD MONTAGE" Heart Collage by Bob Sluys. One day, as I was recovering from my third surgery and limited with my activities, I took all of my get well cards, and cut them up—looking for interesting colors and graphics. It was the ultimate prednisone-fueled project, one that took me several days. I wanted a memento of what I thought would be my last procedure!*

Bob Sluys

A Special Thanks To My Kickstarter Project Supporters!

Writing a cheezy "thank you" would be just that-cheezy! And so, I'll just say that I'm humbled by your interest in and financial support of not only this book, but of me. Whatever happens with this book happens— the thing that matters is people uniting for a common goal even if it's not their own. My story could have been your story. Thank you for letting me tell it.
. . . in no particular order . . . my gratitude goes out equally to:

Jon Botten David Hoskin

Wil de Bakker Mark Stockwell

Joy Bonner Larry & *Priscilla* Larsen

Kathie Larsen Terry Kyriss Shauna Za' Shikany

Martha Bertucci The Arnsbergs Daniel J Mohler Jeffrey Lamrouex

Edward Calder *Carolyn Esparza* Joey B Jewell *Marietta Floor Sharp*

The Shalev's *Amy Lucas* Marcel de Bakker *Teri Olson* Ross Lambert

Rustan Leino *Stacey Piersa* *Tam Katzin* Marc Kane *Barb Boettcher*

Wilten Haynes *Corri* & Wim van Loon Jim Kallimani John Haferbecker

Angelina Hopson Aaron Weisblatt Jeff Herrmann *Donna Hodge*

Robert J Newton *Marlyss McElroy* Mark Peltier *Diane deJong*

Mandi Whiteley Bruce Garnitz Larry Piersa Gary Linstead

Mike Gymnaiates Edward Zabinski Theo & *Marry* Sluys

Richard Dahl *Teri Brenkus* Mike Leslie *Kristen Mylet*

Kellie Rosinski Mark DeVos *Debbie Robinson*

David Longoria *Lynn Pratt* Dean Barker

Kevin Seeley Dean Krippaehne

David Dyrseth *Carma Dreyfus*

Joey Furlan Jeff Devos

The Bringhurst's

Gene Pierce

Straight
From My
Heart

BUTTER*FLIES*

"Are you nervous?", asked Angi . . . "nah, not really . . . well, maybe just a little bit," I lied.

She knew.

6 a.m. June 17, 1994 . . . I had just changed into a standard issue hospital gown, you know, the one-size fits all that ties in the back and doesn't quite close all the way.

I was starved and dying of thirst, but I couldn't have anything to eat or drink—not even water to brush my teeth. A nurse came into the cubicle and handed me a pill, something to make me relax and drowsy, she said. How funny, I thought. They wake you up at five a.m.—just to give you a sleeping pill? Crazy. A few minutes later I was on a gurney being wheeled to pre-op.

The elevator door opened and out stepped my friend Robert, who had gotten up at one a.m. to drive to Seattle from Salem,

Oregon. Little did we know that he'd be making the same trip more than once.

I had told the rest of my family and friends that there was no point in being there so early—besides, I'd taken them out to dinner the night before to enjoy what was to become a regular event known as "The Last Supper". I said my goodbyes to Angi and Robert and was wheeled into pre-op.

The butterflies were starting to flap their wings and head down the runway. The anesthesiologist introduced himself and got to work.

This wasn't really happening, I thought. But it *was* happening, after 15 long years, I was finally having my open . . . heart . . . surgery.

I was the only patient in pre-op. The room was chilly and I was shivering. Cold or nerves. Probably both.

The ceiling was covered with pictures of warm tropical beaches and brightly colored birds and plants. Here's an idea, I remembered thinking—instead of pictures of warm beaches, why not just turn up the freakin' heat?

As I started to drift, I felt a sharp pinch and sting in my wrist and heard the doctor say "missed it" . . . missed what? It sure felt like he'd hit something!

My mind was spinning—trying to ignore the needles that were being stuck in me, saying little prayers asking God for strength and courage, talking myself into that this was a gonna be a piece of cake . . .

The last thing I remembered was an extremely hairy dark-skinned man starting to shave my chest . . . and for some reason I thought that that was *so* funny . . .

CONTENTS

POINT GUARD

It's not often in one's life that we experience something so extraordinary that it becomes unprecedented. Maybe even world-class . . . certainly . . . once-in-a-lifetime.

We all have once-in-a-lifetime experiences—right? Our birth and death for starters. But even though they're once-in-a-lifetime to ourselves, these are common to everybody.

What makes me so special? Not much—other than having the dubious distinction of surviving not just one open heart surgery—but four.

Which of course begs the question—it's no longer once-in-a-lifetime if it happens repeatedly . . . right?

Fine—we'll make it four-in-a-lifetime.

Every year over half-a-million people can look forward to undergoing open heart surgery.

Could you be next?

My name is Bob and I'm not fat, I never smoked and I always got plenty of exercise—yet, in a span of three decades I underwent four separate open heart surgeries. Unprecedented? They were to me.

Now, why would you want to read about someone else's lifetime spent preparing for, enduring, surviving and recovering from four heart surgeries?

Are you kidding? The medical profession. Family. Faith. McDonald's. Death. Incompetence. Sex. Forgiveness—what could be more interesting and entertaining than that?

If you're looking for *Chicken Soup For The Heart Surgery Patient's Soul*—well, you've chosen the wrong book. And this isn't *Eating Fried Chicken Causes Clogged Arteries So It's All Your Own Fault,* either.

If you've already had heart surgery, then this is your story as well. Facing heart surgery? Here's a perspective that I promise your doctor will never give you. Want to avoid having heart surgery . . . at ALL COST? Then this is a must read.

Thirteen years to write and a lifetime to live . . . this is straight from my heart.

—Bob Sluys, March, 2013.

As the Von Trapp family used to sing . . . "Let's start from the very beginning" . . .

WHAT ABOUT BOB? 1

Since I'm pretty much unknown—ah, who am I kidding—I'm a **complete unknown**; allow me just a couple of pages to introduce myself. Thanks!

July 20, 1956 in the city of The Hague, Netherlands. That was my beginning.

I drew my first breath, which I believed was utilized for lots of crying, as the second child and first son to Theo and Marry (Outjers) Sluys (Sluys rhymes with house). My first achievement, major or otherwise was the fact that July 20 was also my fathers' birthday—that's right; I was one birthday present that couldn't be returned.

In 1961 my parents packed up their three kids (six year-old sister Irene, myself right before my fifth birthday and soon to be aged three brother Pete) and crossed the ocean to the land of opportunity, The United States of America.

Like our Pilgrim trailblazers we came over on a ship. The trip took over a week and all I remember is my sister getting an ear infection and seeing some big green statue of a lady holding a torch standing in the water.

It certainly can't be very easy to move away from your home, and leaving behind family, friends and loved ones travel on a ship across an ocean with three toddlers under the age of six to a strange new land whose language you don't speak . . . all to start a new life. Oh, and once we got to Ellis Island in New York, it was another five days or so to get to Seattle, Washington on a Continental Trailways bus, in the blast furnace that is the Midwest during the summer.

Maybe it was at this early age and through my folks that I developed my sense of adventure that has become my nomadic and entrepreneurial way of life throughout the years— sometimes resulting in amazing experiences, and at other times leaving me staring survival straight in the face.

My dad was a pastry chef by trade . . . years later we gave him the nickname "Col. Klink", in honor of the inept and bumbling commander of Stalag 13 of televisions' Hogan's Heroes fame. It was the bald head and accent that did it—not the inept bumbling—and he always played along with a jovial "disssssmisssssssssed"!

Like most people I don't remember much before the age of three. I understand, though, that I was fairly high-maintenance —lots of crying and such. Damn, not a lot of growth there! I remember getting run over by a bicycle and that it hurt like hell. Might as well start at an early age . . . right?

Looking back through the old family photo albums I saw that crew cuts (performed by my father with some sort of flo-bee apparatus) were the hair-style of choice up to grade four, when I went for the "Elvis" look using tube after tube of Brylcreem— just a little dab will do ya!

Well, after a couple of years in the States—my dad had gotten a job working as a pastry chef in the flight kitchen at United Airlines and my mom did various odd jobs such as cleaning apartments and working at an egg farm—my parents finally achieved their dream afforded by this great country—they bought a bakery, and soon *Dutch Pastry Shop* provided the citizens of Edmonds, Washington with the best "Four Loaves For A Dollar" bread and "A Baker's Dozen Donuts" anyone with four quarters could ever want.

Irene, myself and Pete—circa 1962—getting an early start at being a ham!

It was 1963 and things were good! The Beach Boys had just released "Surfin' USA" and before long my brother Pete, pounding out primal beats on an empty Quaker Oats box and myself on a cardboard cutout guitar playing "toes on the nose" guitar riffs were jamming along with Brian, Carl, Dennis and the rest of the gang.

I joined the Cub Scouts and sold light bulbs door to door to raise money for summer camp, once returning home from a successful day of selling only to pee in the pants of my Cub Scout uniform—my mom had been vacuuming the house and hadn't heard the doorbell ring.

I later became a Boy Scout, never noticing if any of our leaders were gay. In fact, I was a late bloomer in the ways of the world—sex, drugs, rock 'n roll—I eventually caught up and made up for lost time—and usually with a nice Cabernet.

Pete and I were close; playing outside, climbing trees and riding bikes. All we needed were friends named Lumpy and Eddie, and you'd have had Wally & The Beav.

I loved reading MAD magazine and drawing my own cartoons. Pete and I even published our very own newspaper: The Sluys Gazette, I think we called it. Pounded out on an old typewriter it contained family news like "Mom and Dad spent $36 on this week's groceries. It took nine bags to hold" . . . pretty earth-shattering info, uh?

I was a huge BATMAN TV show fan. Pete and I made a Batcave out in the woods and set about fighting crime and saving humanity. Actually, we set about *committing* crime.

There were some kids in the neighborhood that we hung out with—I must've been about nine or so, with them being a couple of years older.

Before we knew it we were smoking (puffing on, actually) cigarettes and pipes that we shoplifted from the local 7-11. We also lifted candy and ice cream. I think that we even formed a gang and named it The Rat-Finkz.

As crazy as this might sound, we really were pretty good kids. My parents taught good morals and ethics and even though Pete and I knew it was wrong to steal, we got caught up with some hooligans! I know, I know . . .

Within a couple of weeks our crime spree came to a screeching halt when Pete was busted—and in addition to incurring the wrath of our parents we had to repay our thefts by working at the store, sweeping and such. Lesson learned.

When Beatlemania swept the country in 1964–65 Pete and I would play along with their Saturday morning cartoon series— him on his empty Quaker Oats box and myself on my cardboard cutout guitar. It's funny, but how could I possibly have imagined at that time that most of my adult life would be spent as a musician traveling the world playing many of those same Beatle songs on my bass guitar?

Summer breaks were spent outside playing baseball and going to the elementary school where there was a recreation program headed up by my favorite teacher of all time.

Mr. Rankin T. Kaut.

He stood about six foot four, loved sports and was no nonsense. None. Nada. Zilch. Zip. Pete and I both had him as our fifth grade teacher, and I thought that he was the greatest.

Back in those days a teacher could still command respect and dish out discipline without fear of some parent or organization suing them. And Mr. Kaut had both bases well covered. Disrupt class? (Guilty many, many times) Screw around? (Ditto) Well, you'd better be prepared for some discipline. And, he had a couple of helpers in the discipline department, both of which were named after then currently popular TV shows.

One of them was *Combat*. *Combat* was the rubber sole of an old tennis shoe (Converse Chuck Taylor All-Star I believe), and when it made contact with your open palm or bent-over rear end, well, let's just say it would bring a tear to your eye.

Now *Rat Patrol* was a wooden paddle that made your granny's wooden spoon or Sister Mary's ruler look like a toothpick. If you were unfortunate enough to be on the receiving end of Mr. Kaut's booming directive: "Sluys, grab your ankles", then you could expect the following.

First, the humiliating thousand mile journey from your desk to the front of the classroom. Dead man walking.

Like a condemned prisoner on his way to the gallows you

would slowly trudge down the aisle, cheeks burning with embarrassment and fear. The rest of the class would react in various ways. The wise-ass jocks (yes, they exist even in the fifth grade) would snicker under their breath—gleeful in your misery, even though most of them would soon suffer the same fate.

Most of the girls would look on with sorrow and pity, never having experienced what was about to come. The rest of the class who hadn't experienced corporal punishment would look on in wonder and awe, blissfully unaware of how truly painful this was going to be.

Pain.

My first of many experiences with it.

Mr. Kaut would greet you at the front of the class, looking much much taller than his already 6'4''—and depending on the severity of your infraction would've brought with him either Combat or, heaven forbid . . . be strong, Robert, and whatever you do, don't cry. Bite your lip, and pucker your butt cheeks . . . it's . . . Rat Patrol.

And so it would go. You'd bend over, grab your ankles (it's amazing how flexible you are in the fifth grade), close your eyes, hold your breath and . . . shwoooooooooosh . . . whack!

For all of the butt cheek puckering and lip biting and what not, that paddle on your ass hurt like a sonofabitch. The hairs on the back of my neck would be at full attention, the tips of my ears burning with shame.

And in some strange way, I loved it. Don't get me wrong, I didn't like it but I'd screwed up, so I had to pay the price. Simple. Discipline, it has become a lost art, and I believe it's sorely needed.

Thank you, Mr. Kaut—oh, by the way—try that today? We'll see you in the slammer!

To sum up my early years—all in all they were just fine. Sure, moving to a foreign country at the age of five and not speaking the language was certainly an early-age negative experience that left it's mark, and getting laughed at by kids for "talking funny" wasn't, well, very funny.

Neither was having a last name that rhymes with "louse"—as in "Sluys the Louse", or being called out of my classroom twice a week for speech lessons.

So, basically I had as normal of a childhood you could want. There certainly wasn't any physical abuse or alcoholic parents or things of that nature. Nah, the thing that would really turn my life upside down was still developing . . . inside of me.

I remember one summer vacation, I think it was before 8th grade, that I had planters warts on the bottom of both feet. My folks took me to see Dr. Koome, who was also from the old country, and he proceeded to cut them out of both feet. Not only did it hurt like hell, but I couldn't walk for weeks !!! Why not do one foot at a time? That was my introduction to dubious medical care.

In high school, I was on the track team. Sometimes, after a tough race, it seemed that I couldn't catch my breath as easily as I wanted to. I didn't think too much of it.

I do vaguely remembered my folks telling me that I had a heart murmur, diagnosed at birth. The doctor in Holland had told them that it was a quite common condition and that I would soon outgrow it . . . a heart murmur . . . hmmm . . .

This might be a good place to describe my characteristics and personality . . . my DNA.

I'm the first to admit that I'm not for everyone—who is? But, it's not my fault because I'm Dutch! Haha . . . I'm very logical, honest, direct and can be quite stubborn.

I'm creative with music, video, writing; and I have a quirky sense of humor. I have no time for, well, idiots. I abhor injustice. I can't watch the Sound Of Music or ET without

bawling like a baby, but have no problem busting incompetence
—especially my own.

I'll take the road less traveled every time—conforming to the
norm just never seemed very interesting to me. I don't want to
be like anybody else. Except for maybe Brad Pitt.

I believe I have a strong moral compass and am very loyal. I
have accepted Christ as my savior yet I struggle with giving up
complete control to him.

Some of those qualities have served me well, and some have
almost destroyed me.

I was an average student—school was boring. I gave my
teachers plenty of grief with my quick and clever wit—my
words, not theirs—and my dad bailed me out on more than one
occasion.

It was in the 8th grade at age 13 that I became a Christian. I
was very active at Highlands Community Church and count
Pastor Wilson and Larry Larsen amongst pillars that helped
shape my life.

I graduated high school in 1974 and almost immediately
went on the road, playing trumpet for Country/Western
superstar Roy Clark. The next few years saw me play in several
bands and attend college. Other than the tour with Roy, nothing
too unusual or exciting.

However, the fun is about to begin!

Fasten your seat belts . . .

". . . Of D.B. Cooper, airline food, Adam & Eve . . . and needles."

CONGENITAL
AORTIC STENOSIS 2

1978. I was 22 years old.

The traveling musician bar band routine had gotten old, and since I had always been interested in airplanes and flying, I started to take some flying lessons with hopes of a new career in aviation.

As a kid, especially during summer vacations my brother Pete and I would often spend time at Sea-Tac airport . . . my mom worked the swing shift at Northwest Airlines—she was a cook in the flight kitchen— flight kitchen?

Haha . . . yes! Flight kitchens were places where airlines would prepare food that they would serve on flights—it's true! These were the pre-bag o' peanuts days—hey! —wanna mess with a flight attendant? When they hand you that bag of peanuts, hold it up to your ear, shake it and with a look of concern on your face proclaim that "it sounds like there's one missing" . . . they LOVE that!

Anyway, my mom would go to work around one o'clock and my dad would get off of work at around three o'clock— from

HIS job at the . . . UNITED airlines flight kitchen where he was a "pastry man" as he called it.

We'd go along and for about an hour or so my brother and I would hang out at the airport. These were the *Leave It To Beaver* days—propellor planes, travelers wearing suits and ties, it was an age of innocence—heck, Lucy and Ricky had yet to push their beds together!

We would watch planes take off and land and it was just plain COOL! Plus, being from Holland, we would always travel back to visit relatives and when you work for an airline, buddy passes and other traveling privileges became the norm. Needless to say, I logged hundreds of hours in the air and developed my love of flying.

Oh—check this out: on November 24, 1971, my mom was working her normal shift at Northwest Airlines when word came in that one of their planes had been hijacked— and that the (soon to become) legendary hijacker D.B. COOPER demanded, amongst $200,000 in unmarked bills, parachutes and other things . . . food! Which my mom prepared!!!

This event captured the imagination of the world and to this day this remains unsolved. What if they had only served bags of peanuts back then? How would ol' D.B. have reacted? Folks—the implications are enormous—the very course of history could've been altered! . . . uh, where was I?

OK—when obtaining your pilot's license, you must take a pretty thorough physical. I went to see a doctor who promptly told me that he detected a fairly pronounced heart murmur. Oh yeah, the one my folks had told me I would outgrow. I wasn't concerned—yet. He sent me to see a cardiologist. Dr. Block.

Dr. Block immediately identified the murmur and explained that I would need some tests, and shortly thereafter I experienced my first of many procedures to come: The cardio-catheterization. Damn, that sounded pretty scary, and it was. In fact, it still is and always will be.

My sister Irene, who was eight months pregnant with her first child (my nephew Jason), drove me to the hospital. After some basic prep, I had to sign an informed consent form. It basically explained the risks of the procedure, including death from a stroke, infection, bleeding, all sorts of stuff. Well, I certainly wasn't ready for that.

Here's how it went down. First, Dr. Block shaved my pubic region and gave me an injection of painkiller in the leg right next to the groin. Next, he punctured my femoral artery so that they could thread a catheter up into my heart to measure various pressures and blood flows. As a musician I found it quite ironic to notice that the catheter looked just like one of my bass guitar strings.

Since I was awake, I could watch on a monitor as they guided this wire up into my heart. I could also feel it as it was threaded up through my body . . . think the movie *Aliens*—even though it had not been released yet.

The entire procedure took about 45 minutes, after which I was wheeled into a hallway and left there for about 6 hours with a 20 pound sand bag on my groin to put pressure on the wound to help close it. The diagnosis?

Congenital Aortic Stenosis. I was born with a defective heart valve. I had . . . HEART DISEASE.

The childhood murmur that I would "outgrow it" had become something that would change my life forever. Well, I immediately said goodbye to my new career as an Airline Pilot.

I was stunned. Shocked. A million thoughts, emotions, questions swirled through my mind. What did this mean? How did it happen? Would I die? Was there a cure? Lots of questions, but at the time, very few answers.

The Dr. Block assured me that, although it was a serious problem and would need some type of intervention, it could be years before I would need surgery.

Open heart surgery.

Wait a minute, isn't that for old, out of shape people who smoke and eat crap and don't exercise and . . . uh, that wouldn't be any of *you* . . . would it? I was only 22 years old and just starting to live my life! I wasn't fat, I didn't smoke, I worked out . . . it wasn't . . . fair!

Ha, fair . . . I quickly learned that "fair" is where you go look at small farm animals, eat cotton candy and throw up on the Tilt-A-Whirl.

The words "Open Heart Surgery" quickly became an intrusive and invasive mantra—a dull, mental toothache that throbbed 24 hours a day, 7 days a week 52 weeks a year— for the next 15 years.

No matter what I did, there it was—a dissonant, twisted childlike singsong chorus . . . *Open Heart Surgery* . . . *Open Heart Surgery* . . . *Open Heart Surgery* . . . playing basketball? —better take it easy, don't wanna have a coronary . . . *Open Heart Surgery* . . . jumping around on stage playing my bass? —gotta slow down . . . *Open Heart Surgery.*

Even though I kept pretty busy, I could always expect the "Open Heart Surgery" mantra to appear out of nowhere and swirl through my thoughts. I would often wonder what it would be like. How bad would it hurt? Needles . . . I knew there would be lots of needles. And just like Indiana Jones and snakes, I HATED needles.

I came up with little prayers and sayings like "I'm gonna make it;" "I won't bleed very much;" "I'm gonna have strength and courage;" "It'll be a piece of cake" . . . I would repeat them over and over and over. I didn't even know when I was going to have the surgery, but I wanted to condition my mind with positive reinforcement and visualization.

As sick as this might sound, I actually grew accustomed to my condition and would sometimes use it as a conversation piece or as a way to get a little sympathy or attention. I even used it to avoid things like heavy lifting, which as it turns out might have saved my life.

At least once a year, sometimes twice, I would fly to Seattle from Los Angeles where I lived at the time, for a visit with Dr. Block. Things were progressing, but I was nowhere close to any kind of surgery.

One of the first things that I did when all of this came down was to educate myself on Heart Disease—and remember, this was WAY before Al Gore invented the internet. Here's what I discovered:

Statistics clearly show that the nation's number one cause of death is Heart Disease. And I firmly believe, and studies will support the fact, that most heart disease is caused by . . . ourselves.

And if this is a secret then we truly ARE delusional.

Overeating, smoking, stress, not exercising . . . these all point to our lack of accepting responsibility for confronting the issues that affect our lives.

Now don't worry, I'm not going to preach to you about changing your ways (well, maybe a little). I'm just going tell you my story and you can respond anyway you like. Will it make a difference? I don't know, that'll be up to you. After all, remember Adam and Eve? They were told: "Don't eat the apple" . . . and we all know how well THEY listened. And that was GOD talking.

Here are a few things to chew on: nearly one quarter of you

will have one or more forms of cardiovascular disease in your lifetime. And nearly one million of you will die from it . . . THIS YEAR ALONE ! And again next year. And the next. And, the vast majority of those deaths are completely unnecessary!

Imagine no expensive doctor bills, no putting your family thru hell, no getting your body ripped open . . . Of course you can't imagine that unless you've been there. I have.

Oh yeah, I wasn't gonna preach. Sorry.

If you don't eat and drink in moderation, exercise regularly, and, if you smoke or live stressfully than your chances of contracting heart disease are very, very high— but you already know that. Besides, it won't happen to any of you!

The reason I bring this up is because most of the people that I just described will one day have a sudden coronary, get rushed (maybe) to the hospital, have emergency open heart bypass surgery, and wake up (hopefully) going "uh, . . . what happened?"

Here's what happened: Your chest was cracked open and your ribs were spread apart. Your legs were cut from groin to ankle with sections of vein taken out. You had more needles, tubes and catheters stuck in you than a voodoo doll, and you awoke feeling like a Mac truck had hit you.

Oh, and your family went through hell and you've piled up $100,000 or more in doctor and hospital bills, for what?

You see, the bitch for me was that I had over 15 years to think about this, not some 30-minute ambulance ride.

From here on out, my life would never be the same.

 Heart Fact! Heart disease is the No. 1 Killer of Women.

". . . Who would YOU let into your heart? "

USED *SCARS* 3

"**If it were you,** what would you do?" It was my final question, and the one on which my decision would hinge. Not just my decision, but also my future. In fact, maybe even **my life**.

It was early January 1994, and after 15 years in anticipation of an eventual surgical intervention Dr. Block informed me that my aortic valve disease was finally reaching a potentially life threatening stage. Dr. Block referred me to a surgeon who was the Professor and Chief of Cardio-Thoracic surgery at the University of Washington hospital. Dr. Verrier.

Dr. Verrier looked to be in his late forties with lots of unkempt wavy graying hair and piercing eyes. He had certain swagger, almost an east coast vibe to his speech and manner, and the charisma and confidence of a used car salesman. I liked him right away!

Dr. Verrier turned around and walked back towards me. "The Ross Procedure" he said, without hesitation. He answered with

such supreme confidence, yet later, I would wonder many times
if that answer were based on my close resemblance to a Guinea
Pig

*Playing bass in a Paul Revere & The Raiders tribute band in
1979 when I was diagnosed with my aortic stenosis. Wish I
still had that bass . . . and the hair!*

We had earlier spent about an hour going over the various
surgical options that I would have to choose from.

Here's a quick pro and con rundown of each one:

#1. A mechanical valve. Constructed from a composite, it's
the most common replacement valve used, it's usually very
reliable and at that point had about a 15-year track record. The
downside is if one fails, you've got about three minutes to
replace it. They make an audible clicking sound, and, you have
to take a blood thinner every day for the rest of your life. Get in

a wreck, and have some internal bleeding?

Your blood won't clot and you could bleed to death. Hmm, didn't care too much for that one. Oh, and the blood thinner? It has some of the same ingredients in it as rat poison!

#2) A Stentless Porcine Bioprothesis.

Say what? Basically, a pig heart valve. Hey, why not? The benefit with them is that no blood thinners are necessary. The downsides were that they only last seven to ten years due to calcification, one would also develop a strange aversion to ham sandwiches and many patients start stuttering like Mel Blanc with Tourette's Syndrome. Come on—that was funny!

For myself at age 37, not such a good option; why, I could be looking at three or four more operations! (Insert loud, theatrical coughing sound.)

A couple of other choices included a stented bioprothesis and an aortic homograft, neither of which seemed very viable after closer examination.

That left the Ross Procedure.

First performed during the 1960's by a British doctor for whom it's named, in concept it seems like the perfect solution especially for younger patients and for women who later wanted to have children.

Briefly, here's how it goes down. Your diseased aortic valve is removed. They then harvest (remove) your own healthy pulmonary valve. Since your pulmonary valve is almost identical to your aortic valve, they now move it over and use it to replace your diseased aortic valve. They then use an irradiated cryo-preserved donor valve harvested from a cadaver to put in your pulmonary position.

As complicated as that sounds, the theory behind it is quite simple. You get a new aortic valve from the best possible source: yourself. And since the stress, function and pressure on the pulmonary valve is much less than the aortic, the cadaver donor valve should work fine. So simply put, there's no blood thinners to have to take and since they're both human tissue, they should last a lifetime.

So why wasn't the Ross Procedure the procedure of choice? Here's the problem. After a promising start with the Ross Procedure, people starting dying right and left, but the doctors at that time couldn't identify the problem and the Ross Procedure quickly went the way of the dinosaur.

After about 20-25 years, the problem was discovered: an important artery was inadvertently being damaged, and just like Jurassic Park, the Ross Procedure started to make a comeback, although it still remained quite uncommon and infrequently used.

As Dr. Verrier gave his answer, he fixed his steely gaze on me, and I knew instantly what my choice would be.

Here's some unsolicited advice: always, always, always, always ask a doctor how much experience they have with the procedure that they're going to perform on you. I didn't ask. I was so pumped and he was so convincing. I later found out that I would be only his seventh Ross Procedure patient—hardly an experienced veteran performing a difficult operation.

By the way, in a letter dated a few days later, Dr. Verrier thanked Dr. Block for the referral and mentioned several times how much he enjoyed meeting me. He also said that I should do superbly and that he would expect an excellent result. Mark those words.

 Healthy Heart Secret! Eat LESS, Exercise MORE . . .

". . . In this chapter our hero (me!) will help you digest a topic that was featured 10 years later in Morgan Spurlock's acclaimed documentary "Super Size Me" —proving once again our hero's (mine!) pioneering ways for the betterment of all humanity."

DID *SOME*BODY SAY MC*BYPASS?* 4

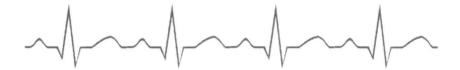

Here's a little McNugget to nibble on: Every 60 seconds, 30 acres of rain forest are destroyed in order to raise beef for fast-food restaurants that will sell it to people, giving them strokes and heart attacks which raise medical costs and insurance rates, providing insurance companies with more money to invest in large corporations that branch out further into the third-world so they can destroy more rain forests.

Read that again—I'll wait.

Here's something that still clogs my arteries.

In 1994 I went to Valley Medical Center in Renton, Washington for my pre-surgery cardio-catheterization; also known as an angiogram. Remember, I'd had my first angiogram 15 years earlier when I was first diagnosed.

The doctors needed to get a better look at the anatomy of my heart, including arteries, specifically in the area of the surgery. Since no two hearts are identical, having an artery in the wrong place would not allow them to perform the procedure. To help identify their exact location, Dr. Block would inject a contrast media, or dye, into my heart. It's usually a fairly routine process—unless you have a severe reaction in the form of Anaphylactic Shock and almost die like I did! But—that's detailed in an upcoming chapter entitled "*I am SO screwed.*"

So, they cut a hole in your groin and run a wire up your femoral artery into your heart and inject a dye to see how badly screwed up you are—it's a procedure that many of you can already start looking forward to having! (Be nice, Bob . . .)

Anyway, what do you think that I saw in the lobby of that hospital—other than caring nurses, illegal immigrants working the system for free health care and an overpriced gift shop?

A McDonald's.

That's right: the golden arches of healthy eating—in a hospital. Let's stop for a moment and think about what kind of message that sends out. Sorta like having the cast of The Sopranos presenting anger management seminars.

Actually, it sort of makes sense, if you think about it. After all, why in the world would a hospital want you to be healthy? They'd have nothing to do! Why, they'd go out of business quicker than . . . well, a McDonald's in Bombay!

What that McDonald's really represents is . . . job security! Which is exactly what I was told by a nurse when I asked her "What's up with the McDonald's in your hospital?" And, when I asked Dr. Block about the McDonald's he replied that he wasn't too crazy about a McDonald's in his hospital either, but only because he preferred Burger King. He then said "just kidding." Hmm . . . it must have been his bed-pan delivery. Priceless.

Now, as a four-time graduate of the cardio-care unit, the only possible reason that I can see for having a McDonald's in a hospital is so that visitors can sneak the patients something to eat other than hospital food—believe me, if there's anything that'll kill you quicker than fast food it's hospital food. Since many are probably dying anyway, what's the harm?

In fact, the morning after my *SPOILER ALERT: *third* open heart surgery in Oklahoma City, the nurse slid my breakfast tray onto my stand. I wasn't terribly hungry, but, as I lifted the cover off the plate I lost my appetite completely. There, on my plate was a serving of sausage and biscuits & gravy.

Biscuits & gravy? Are you kidding me?

I was an open heart surgery patient in an intensive care unit —where was my yoghurt and perhaps some Fruity Pebbles?

Biscuits and gravy?

Ahhhh—then it hit me! This was Oklahoma City—and I was just receiving a heapin' helpin' of some good ol' southern hospitality, that's all! I was almost expecting to hear "Ya'll come back now, ya hear" when I checked out.

Hey, they don't waste any time in getting you back in there!

You know what? . . . If I could do it all over, I'd go to college and become a cardiologist. It'd be great! I'd have the media, big business and fast food corporations all providing me with an endless supply of lemmings, er, I mean patients . . . for free!

Why, I'd make millions! I'd never be out of work! Yep, you parents out there owe it to your children to have them become cardiologists. Or authors who write about their heart surgery experiences.

Put down that Quarter Pounder for a moment and think about this:

Hospitals aren't here to educate us or prevent disease. That's our own job. Hospitals exist to fix our screw ups.

Have a little too much to drink? Driving your car? Get in a wreck? Injure or kill a few people? Hey, the E.R. will patch you right up—right?

Smoke a couple a packs a day? For 30 or 40 years? Got a slight case of lung or throat cancer? No biggie, just go to the hospital—they'll cut that stuff right out—doctors LOVE cutting on stuff!

You could even get one of those cool sounding synthesizer voice boxes so that when you talk you'll sound just like that dude on Star Wars—why, the hospital's got it all. Oh, yeah; don't forget to get a hole in your throat so that you can still smoke your cigarette.

Actually, having that McDonald's in the hospital is actually doing you a favor. If you have a coronary while inhaling your Big Mac, the operating room is conveniently located right across the lobby, next to McRonald's Playland—just stagger on over for your quadruple McBypass.

Heck, instead of a quadruple McBypass, why not Supersize it and get a quintuple McBypass?

By the way, when the kid at the drive up window asks if you want that supersized, he's referring to your ass & their corporate profits, not the french fries.

And if you think about it, a McDonald's "Value-Meal" is not quite the value you might think it is once you've factored in the cost of bypass surgery.

You know, their sign outside should really read: Over 30 billion arteries clogged.

So, not believing what I was seeing, I went into the McDonald's for a closer look. Here was their menu—I'm not making this up: Big Mac $2.39, Chicken McNuggets $1.89, Quadruple McBypass $43, 500, . . .

Check this out:

In December of 1999 the Institute of Medicine recommended that Medicare should spend an estimated $1.4 BILLION dollars over the next five years to pay for nutrition counseling to help senior citizens change their diets. Medicare is currently spending $7,200 per person on a pilot program to test whether a low-fat diet can change the prognosis for people who might otherwise need bypass surgery.

Spend $1.4 BILLION dollars to tell people to "cut back on the French Fries." And a study to see if you'd still need open heart surgery if you reduced the amount of crap that you stuffed down your pie hole?

HELLO, ARE WE NUTS !? We don't need to spend billions to do that—do we?

Let's take a little survey, shall we?

How many of you think that eating healthier will reduce the risk of having heart surgery? Well, let's call ol' Uncle Sam with these results, shall we? Maybe they'll give us a cut of that 1.4 BILLION dollars.

And why is the government going to spend $1.4 billion to educate our senior citizens?

Bad habits start at an early age and the older we get, the tougher it is to change, isn't it? Let's not wait to educate the elderly, let's educate the young!

If you want to eat yourself into a coronary go right ahead, but at least step up and give your kids a fighting chance. They can't choose. You can. And the same goes for smoking and exercising.

Imagine what would happen to our lives if we took care of our bodies. We might feel better! Ah, forget it, Bob, that's too much work. Besides, I have issues, man. Remember that cheeseburger? It represents the hugs my mom never gave me. Oh yeah? Tough titty.

And the two packs a day? Well, that was from the time I got dumped by that chick in the 7th grade 'cause I wasn't cool. Listen dude, she was right, you weren't cool, so get over it.

By the way, you'll be happy to know that in October 2000 the McDonald's at Valley Medical Center was closed. (pause) . . . to be replaced by a . . . Burger King?

We really don't need a caption, do we?

 Healthy Heart Fact: Ketchup is NOT a vegetable.

35

" . . . Let's jump into the WayBack Machine for a quick trip to tinsletown . . ."

I *LOVE* L.A. ! 5

Before we start suture' and dicin' I've got to at least pay homage to the 15 years between the diagnosis and my first surgery, besides, aren't ages 22–37 the prime years of one's life?

Let's do this: Even tho' I'm gonna cram a ton of living into a few paragraphs I'll keep it interesting and only discuss the stuff you REALLY want to know about–Hollywood dirt! The inside scoop! In other words—groupies!

Look at what I just wrote—"I'm gonna cram a ton of living into a few paragraphs"—truth is, I crammed a ton of living into those years because I had a newfound sense of urgency. I wasn't fixated on a gloom and doom woe is me I'm gonna die lifestyle—far from it. In fact, I did a shitload of living that I promise most of you couldn't imagine doing in three lifetimes.

Arrogant?

No. Just being honest.

But, let's get to the groupies!

It took some days/weeks/months after my diagnosis for not only the shock to wear off but to slowly get back to a level of activity that I was accustomed to. Here's the deal: I was playing bass guitar in lounge bands. There—I said it. If you're touring with a big name, you have roadies and maybe groupies . . . haha . . . the bands I were in had neither! This is important because with my newly discovered condition I was super wary of lifting stuff! Like my 150 pound Ampeg SVT bass cabinet. And 150 pound chicks.

So—here's the fastest two minutes for recapping 15 years you'll ever read!

1979 found me playing in a Paul Revere and the Raiders tribute band in Portland. Later that year I joined the Steppen' Stonz, being the only white guy in an R&B show group! There's nothing like the smell of 7 sweaty polyester jumpsuits in a tiny dressing room! 1980 I played in a few more Northwest bands— even though I was cautious I slowly kept getting back to my norm—lots of basketball whenever I could, jogging, and, trying to avoid helping my bandmates schlep our equipment . . . hey— maybe that's why I was in so many bands!

SEX, DRUGS AND ROCK 'N ROLL COMMENTARY ALERT!

Part of the stereotype of musicians is true—let's talk drugs. I never did them. Nothing. Except for puffing on a joint and not inhaling a la Bill Clinton when I was with a faith-based group in 1974. That makes me incredibly unique. Folks! This was the 70's and 80's! Coke was the thing! The closest I ever got to Coke was a TV commercial for the drink featuring Kim Carnes that I was in. My heart condition might have SAVED MY LIFE!

With my schnoz, if I had developed a taste for the nose candy, I'd have never made it. So, the worst I did was become a wino—red wine—the healthy kind! Besides, I was saving myself for the REAL deal—why mess around with kid stuff like reefers and coke when you can have trained professionals administer highly-regulated controlled substances like MORPHINE directly into your system via safe and sterile needles whilst you're relaxing in the comfort of your own bed—and it's being paid for by some insurance company! This is beautiful! What a country!

Where was I ? The summer of 1981 found me moving to Los Angeles. For the next 9 years I played in bands, started a video-taping service for the Musicians Union, appeared in several TV shows and movies as a . . . musician! Included was the afore-mentioned 1988 Coke commercial featuring Kim Carnes . . . I pretended to play keyboards and made about $10,000! Don't believe me? You can check it out right here:

 http://www.youtube.com/watch?v=fPT3mjlVZal

—don't blink, you might miss me! Just look for the keyboard player with the hair!

I had a relationship with Joy for a few years. She was/is a very talented singer-songwriter and we worked hard to build a career and get "signed." Getting signed to a record label was everything—after all, how else would anybody ever get to hear your music? However, because of Al Gore and his internet, all you need nowadays is a laptop, some wi-fi, green hair, a coupla nose rings, some tattoos and presto!—you're a rock star! Not that I'm bitter . . . by the way, I had my ears pierced in 1978. Let me repeat: 1978. NO ONE had pierced ears then—for awhile I took a lot of heat for being gay and all that . . . ah, the trials and tribulations of being a fashion trendsetter.

*Straight outta the pages
of TV Guide!*

1982 found me on People's Court. Me and Judge Wapner. I won.

In 1983 I took some time and went to Albuquerque to start a band. The band never happened but I got involved in a highly secretive cult-like society: Scrabble! I ended up playing at a high level and actually even winning money playing in tournaments. In fact, in 2011 I launched a website featuring me teaching Scrabble as my alter-ego/superhero ScrabbleGuy!

Here's another shameless plug, check it out! Really!
http://www.scrabblehelp.net/blog/

All during this time, as active as I was, I was highly attuned to my heart condition and pending (albeit completely unknown as to when) operation. Like the song goes, we're all living to die and dying to live. I was just living the best I could, doing what I enjoyed and was good at. It was a weird and confusing juxtaposition if I stopped to think about it.

1990 found me at 34 years old having decided that my chances for "making it" were slim and none. Truth be told, I never went all in. Wanna make it in show biz? Be ready to give it everything you have 24/7/365 OR, be related to Quincy Jones. I was pretty good in music and worked hard, but it just didn't happen.

Joy surprising me on my 33rd birthday.

Groupies? What groupies! Just me and some friendly gals!

I also needed a change. I moved back to the Seattle area and starting teaching show biz at Green River Community College where I had attended back in 1976. How did I get the gig? Through Pat Thompson, THEIR version of Quincy Jones—see? It's who you know!

Well, kids there ya have it—a little trip down memory lane . . . let's get back to the good stuff!

With Pat Thompson at Don Ho's all you can eat luau buffet in Hawaii-1986 . . . make sure you go through the line before Pat does!

 Healthy Heart Factoid: The Food Pyramid is NOT where the ancient Egyptians kept their grub before the invention of refrigerators.

". . . What doesn't kill you now, eventually will!"

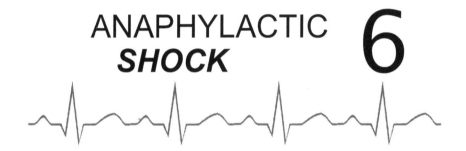

ANAPHYLACTIC *SHOCK* 6

. . . "after wolfin' down a coupla' Egg McMuffins"—just kidding—I was prepped for the catheterization. For maximum effect, and a preview of things to come, here are Dr. Block's official procedure notes, verbatim:

"Following informed consent, the patient was brought to the Special Procedures Room where he was prepped and draped in the usual manner. The right femoral artery area was infiltrated with 2% xylocaine, and a single-wall needle used to puncture the right femoral artery. Over a teflon guide-wire, a 6 french Hemaquet sheath was placed, and the patient was given 2500 units of intra-arterial heparin. A 6 French L4 Judkins catheter was placed and could not cannulate the left coronary ostium. We then placed a 6 French L5 Judkins catheter, and this barely cannulated the left coronary ostium. Injections were made with 6-8 cc of Hypaque 76 and cineangiography performed."

"Following the 3rd injection, the patient began complaining of tightness in his throat, difficulty breathing, and some burning and headache. He had marked edema and facial swelling and blood pressure modestly fell. The catheter was removed from the left coronary ostium. It was felt the patient was suffering a reaction to contrast dye. He was given 25 mg of intravenous Benadryl, 125 mg of intravenous Prednisolone, and an intravenous saline drip was given. Over the next 4-5 minutes, the patient was then given a total of 1.0 mg of intra-arterial epinephrine in incremental doses. His hemodynamics improved, but he was still complaining of throat tightness, although he appeared adequately oxygenated. However, he was peripherally cyanotic. Dr. Dion of Anesthesia was called, and she closely observed the patient over the next 20-30 minutes. The patient was given a total of 4mg of intravenous Versed during this time, and approximately 2 liters of intravenous saline solution through a large bore IV, started by Dr. Dion. He then stabilized.

An R4 catheter was then passed with the aid of a guide wire into the left ventricle, and pressure recorded in the left ventricle and a pullback across the aortic valve. One additional injection was made into the left coronary ostium subsequent to this with Hexabrix. The L4 catheter was removed, and the patient moved to the stretcher for sheath pulling. He had considerable shaking at this time and was given an additional 2 mg of intravenous Versed. The sheaths were pulled, and at this point the patient was stable with his anaphylactic reaction slowly resolving. He was transferred back to the ambulatory unit in stable condition."

So, what exactly did all of that mean?

Well, first of all, in Dr. Block's own words, "that was the worst case of anaphylactic reaction I've ever seen. You almost died, Bob." "Almost died?" Wait a minute—I haven't even had my surgery yet!

As for the "tightness in the throat", that felt like I was being strangled. And, "some burning and headache?" Imagine what it might feel like to have a boiling hot liquid poured into your bloodstream, a stinging, burning, itching sensation running throughout your entire body. "Considerable shaking?" Yeah, like the chills you get when you have the flu or stub your toe.

After all of that, I don't recall. The Versed mentioned by Dr. Block is a drug given during procedures that acts as a short term amnesiac. I do understand that I was out for quite some time.

I remember that when I awoke, Angi was there and seemed very worried as she explained to me what had happened. I also remember that my fingers were plumped up like Ball Park Franks.

After about 4–5 hours of lying still with a heavy sandbag on my groin, which was used to apply pressure to help close the wound, Angi and I went home, and two days later I was back on my feet as I videotaped the wedding of my friends Pat and Mette-Lisa. Afterwards, we went to a local seafood restaurant and I ordered a shellfish dish. What a dummy, shellfish can also cause toxic shock reaction like I had just had. And even though Angi warned me, well, I can be quite stubborn. Fortunately, the only shock that I experienced that night was when the bill arrived. Badump-bump . . .

Even though I was pumped full of Versed, the vivid memories of my episode with Anaphylactic Shock will always remain with me.

 Healthy Heart Fact: A "hearty" meal is anything but.

. . ."I blame it all on my name—I shoulda stuck with Robert"

SHISH-KA-*BOB* 7

So, how many of you have had open heart surgery? If so, what was your favorite part—other than going home?

Well, mine was the Shish-ka-BOB! Actually, it's officially known as a Foley catheter. Allrighty, let's get the squirming party started!

It was 6 a.m.—the first morning post-surgery. After a night of drifting in and out of sleep I was awaken by a nurse and her assistant. She asked me how I felt.

Let me stop right there: Even in my groggy state, I heard her loud and clear, but I wasn't quite sure how to answer, cuz I'd never felt like that before. And, even though you're pumped full of morphine and who knows what else, there's still a sensation quite unlike anything else I'd ever experienced. Basically, it felt like I'd taken a beating like in one of those Batman movies.

Being on morphine, which by the way is warm and smooth, having your chest cracked open still hurts. Another thing about morphine—at least for me—it doesn't make the pain go away per se, it's almost like it makes you not care.

Well, as I slowly started to regain my senses I noticed that the nurse was an extremely attractive blonde and her assistant was a young man approximately seven feet ten inches tall. Let's call him Lurch—remember him from The Addams Family?

She announced that she had good news! It was time to remove my Foley catheter. That's not good news, it's winning the friggin' lottery!

What's a Foley catheter, you might ask. A Foley catheter is a clear plastic tube, like the kind in an aquarium, which is inserted into your bladder (by way of the penis, guys—the INSIDE of the penis). It keeps you from peeing all over everything when you're out. I will from now on refer to it as the Shis-ka-BOB . . . in honor of me! Fortunately, they put it in after you're already knocked out. Even in my grogginess that did seem like good news, indeed.

Well, the nurse pulled back my sheet, checked out the scene, put on some gloves, performed some preparation and instructed me to exhale on the count of three. Oh, she also mentioned that I might experience "a little discomfort."

Now here's a quick course in medical terminology: "A little discomfort" really means "A lot of pain"—if not physical, than certainly, especially in this instance, MENTAL!

Well, on the count of three, out came the tube.

Let me stop right there. That experience alone should be enough to lay off the Krispy Kremes for a day or two, ok?

Let me stop again. I might normally not object if a beautiful blond wants to get up, er, close and personal, however, I found that experience to be somewhat humiliating, even in a hospital setting.

QUICK TIP: When going in for your surgery, check your dignity, pride and modesty in at the reception desk—you won't be needing them.

Secondly, her assistant seemed WAY too interested in the whole affair.

And now for the fun part.

After the tube came out, the nurse said . . ."I need you to pee."

Ok.

She then handed me a container.

"Now?" I asked.

"Yes, if you would," she replied.

They both turned their heads and left me to my own devices, so to speak.

I couldn't go. Nothing. Not a drop.

I reported my failure and the nurse said "Well, you really need to get all of those fluids out of your body, so you'll have to keep trying."

I still couldn't go.

At that point the nurse said "I'm sorry, but if you haven't gone by 7 o'clock, I'll need to reinsert the catheter." In a complete panic, I looked up at the clock. 6:25.

No, not the Shis-Ka-BOB, not while I'm awake. This couldn't be happening to me!

She suggested I visualize peeing. Good idea! I tried, it didn't work. I glanced up at the clock: 6:30—I had a half an hour. She ran some water. No good. 6:35—She put my hand in a bowl of warm water. Not a drop—talk about performance anxiety. I looked up at the clock again: 6:40.

I then heard a high-pitched feminine voice—it was Lurch, asking me if he/she could help. Now I REALLY launched into full-scale panic mode!

At that point the nurse said they'd be back at 7 o'clock, and they left the room.

I sat on the edge of my bed and did everything I could to pee. Well, some things just aren't meant to pee, er, I mean be.

Promptly at 7a.m. they returned, and as promised, your ol' buddy Bob got re-Shish-Ka-BOBBED.

The quick 1,2,3 and out she comes from an hour earlier was now a centimeter by millimeter journey of a thousand miles.

For fun, here's what you can try at home to experience the same sensation. Grab a length of . . . on second thought, that might not be a good idea . . .

Is there a lesson in all of that? Well, actually I imagine that sometimes when we want something soooo bad, we try too hard instead of just relaxing and going with the flow.

I only wish that I'd had a flow to go with.

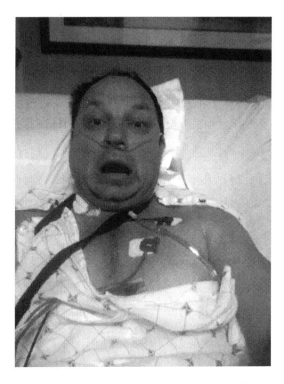

NO! I don't care WHO it's named after!
ANYTHING but the Shish-Ka-BOB!

"Darn it—I can never remember what I forgot!"

I *REMEMBER* 8

I was slowly starting to **regain my senses**. After the harrowing experience with the Shish-ka-BOB, I was faced with the not so pleasant and challenging task of recovery. At first it's mainly just a lot of resting and sleeping, although it's not really sleeping in the conventional sense. It's more like . . . drifting in and out of being coherent.

Some of my memories include signing a consent form the day before the surgery that stated there's a 1 to 5% chance that you could die from complications, infection, a stroke, and/or other such pleasantries.

Hey, people win the lottery all of the time, and those odds are 1 in 7 million, so 1 out of 20 is nothing to fool around with. Listen up; don't mess around with ANY surgery if you can avoid it. And you can.

I was informed that in addition to my valve replacement Ross Procedure they had discovered a large five-centimeter aneurysm in my aorta. The surgeon patched it with a Dacron sleeve. My brother Pete recalled that when Dr. Verrier came out of the operating room to update everyone on my progress he felt enormous anxiety when the aneurysm was mentioned. After all, it could have burst at any time in all of those preceding years while we were playing hoops, and Pete said that he would have felt horrible if that had happened.

Yeah, me too!

My room was located in a wing of the hospital called 5 NE—I was on the 5th floor of the North East tower. I mention this cuz over the years, whenever I would have a meal with my folks and my mom ordered something unhealthy— which was quite often —I would blurt out "five northeast." It quickly became a buzz word for anything unhealthy. I'd come over for dinner and ask what we were having—"five northeast" would always be the response. French Fries at Mickey Dee's became "five northeast" . . . if you think about it, joking around about heart surgery is kind of morbid, but people act strangely in stressful circumstances. Trust me.

My mom, me and Angi—right after The Last Supper—and the night before round #1. Still hamming it up....

The night before my surgery, after our "Last Supper", Angi and I went to our room at the University Motor Lodge—since we lived about an hour and a half from the hospital and had to be there at 6 am, we thought it would make more sense to stay across the street. Before hitting the hay I thoroughly washed myself with a special soap, concentrating my chest area. I slept peacefully—as I did before every surgery. Once you're all in, there's no reason to toss and turn!

So-what *was* recovery like? Well, since you asked . . .

I remember family and friends hovering over me in the I.C.U. They resembled giant demented clown heads with big leering grins, going in and out of focus, their speech sounding like some deranged out-of-control calliope from a B movie.

I remember the TV being on and watching the infamous O.J. Simpson White Ford Bronco chase and thinking, please don't get shot. I felt quite differently a couple years later as I watched the verdict from the trial of century being read.

I remember a doctor bringing his class in to discuss my case, and feeling like an exhibit in some freak show.

I remember the constant visits by the needle lady who would draw fresh blood samples for the lab. What had once been my biggest fear had become routine—and to this day I don't even think twice about getting stuck. Mainly because it just doesn't hurt! It's all in our heads!

I remember having to perform hourly breathing exercises with a spirometer—a device that helps to keep your lungs clear. It was hard. At first.

I remember the room being extremely hot and I remember the sour stench of my sweaty body. In part I understand that the morphine I was receiving had something to do with that.

I remember waking at four in the morning to watch the Dutch soccer team lose yet another World Cup.

I remember having my chest tube removed. The chest tube is used to drain fluids from the cavity around your heart. After a couple of days the excess fluids are pretty much gone and so out comes the tube. It doesn't hurt per se, but like most medical procedures it's the unknown, the anticipation of something unpleasant to happen.

I remember the time when I had a pain near my heart, probably from my chest tube poking against something that it shouldn't have been. It was excruciating. I remember yelling and screaming "help me" for what seemed like hours—each breath triggering a new jolt of pain, er, sorry, uh, I mean "discomfort."

I remember my friends Larry and Teresa being there to see this, and feeling embarrassed and helpless. Them and me.

I remember the nurse telling me that she couldn't give me any more Morphine, and that the Doctor would be back in 45 minutes.

I remember those 45 minutes feeling like an eternity.

Quick note: If you have a major surgery be sure to ask for a machine that allows you to self medicate. You can't overdose, but it will let you administer pain medication as needed. For whatever reason I was not given this option.

I will always remember and be thankful that Robert came up from Salem to be there for me. I later heard that he kept the waiting room (if not the entire hospital) entertained with his famous balloon animals and not so famous jokes. And all that time I thought people were busy just talking about what a great guy I was and how they felt so bad for me and that they wished it were them instead . . .

I remember a nurse, an elderly lady named Audrey, who normally didn't work in cardiac, picking up the container holding the fluids that had taken 2 days to drain from my chest one drop at a time. I remember watching most of what was in the tube pour right back into my body.

I remember nurse Audrey later spilling a bag of IV fluid on Angi's dress.

I remember Dr. Verrier's many visits to check up on me, each time tugging on my big toe and exclaiming "Beautiful, beautiful."

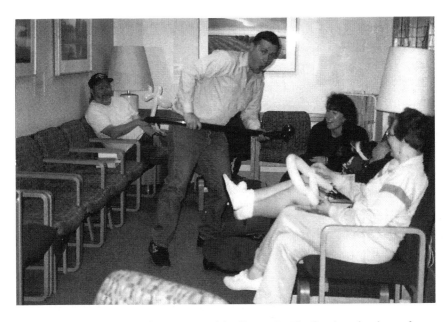

Robert working the room—I believe that's the beginning of his famous black poodle dog balloon animal hat that he's making! Where's the reverence? The humanity?

I also remember a few months later after my (spoiler alert!) second surgery that Dr. Verrier was nowhere to be seen. My toe still misses him . . .

I remember two students of mine stopping by and bringing me a latte. My heart rate was about 120 bpm—I certainly didn't need any caffeine, but, hey, it tasted great! Besides, in Seattle drinking a latte is akin to a religious ritual.

I remember having to clutch a pillow to my chest whenever I coughed—and just being able to draw shallow, whimpery breaths. A one year old's birthday cake would've been safe.

I remember having to learn how to get in and out of bed without using my arms to push off. Just for shits and giggles give that a try it sometime.

I remember my first steps. Slow and unsteady.

I remember my mom getting upset with Angi for not giving up her seat so that she could sit next to her son's bed.

I remember being taken to a small room with three other much older and obviously out of shape men to watch a really retarded video on the recovery process once you got home.

*Suggestion to the medical community:
With all of the time that family and friends have waiting during surgery and while visiting, why not create an instructional video for THEM to watch. Recovery is not just some tissue healing. It involves everybody —family and friend alike—and yet there seems to be little if any information for them, outside of a few pamphlets. Nobody reads those. Here's a chance to provide some needed help in the recovery process.

Although it wasn't a week at the Maui Ritz–Carlton I remember feeling safe and secure while I was there—and after four days, it was time to go home.

Amazing—in the 1950's, President Eisenhower suffered a heart attack and spent six weeks in bed. I had open heart surgery and went home in four days! In fact, I like to joke that the first card I received was from my HMO—it read "At $10,000 per day, we hope you go home REAL soon–we're sending a limo!"

My friend Pat picked me up and drove me home in a borrowed mini-van, comfortable and easy to get in and out of. We stopped for lunch at one of my favorite restaurants and I had fettuccini and a glass of wine. Hey, it was time to celebrate my "new life" with a real meal!

I was very tired by the time I got home. I sat down on the couch and just as I started to fall asleep, my folks stopped by and wanted to visit. I heard Angi explain that I was exhausted and needed to rest. I also heard my mom reply "But we drove all the way over to see him and couldn't she just wake me."

I'll just say this: Going through a major procedure like open heart surgery is tough enough without having to deal with any B.S. It's not that I didn't want to hang out with them, and I always appreciated people's concern—besides, I'm usually a ton of fun to hang with!— but this is a time when your needs must come first, and those around you must be willing to understand and accept that. After all, someday, according to the statistics, it'll happen them!

I'm not going to go into too many details here, but over the next couple of years I experienced many instances of what I perceived to be selfish and insensitive behavior through acts and comments—from family, friends and most surprisingly, from medical professionals.

That first night home I awoke at about 2 a.m. to go to the bathroom. As I finished, I looked in the mirror. It was hot, so I wasn't wearing a shirt. There it was. The scar.

Almost a foot long. Red and angry. Standing there looking at it, a slow realization started to sink in. It had happened. After 15 years, it had finally happened. I'd had my long awaited open heart surgery and I'd . . . survived!

Thank you, Jesus!!!!!!!!

I started to cry. Not a cloudburst of tears, or a loud emotional display—just a quiet sobbing. I didn't know why, but I felt sad, afraid, happy, uncertain, confident, every emotion, and all at the same time. For all of those years I had bottled up my feelings, had never cried, had always wanted to maintain a positive frame of mind, to be a strong example. And now, it was all coming out, and I was letting loose and letting go.

After a few minutes I crawled back into bed, Angi comforted me, and I settled into a deep, deep sleep.

HEART SURGERY 101: I may be just a bass player and such, but to me, there are TWO kinds of heart surgery—open heart and open CHEST.

MOST heart surgeries are for bypass—your arteries are clogged and you need to bypass them—Bill Clinton, David Letterman, Larry King; list goes on and on . . . well, they for whatever reason needed bypass surgery. Bypass surgery does not open the heart like VALVE replacement surgery. Valve replacement is a completely different and more involved and invasive procedure.

So—not to diminish one's experience with open CHEST surgery, but, until you've had a valve job . . .

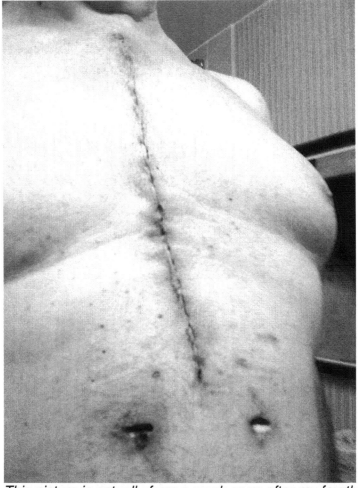

This picture is actually from a week or so after my fourth surgery in December of 2011. Notice the two chest tube holes. Amazingly within just a few months the scars are barely visible!

 Heart Fact: The average heart beats 100,000 per day—and a lot less frequently when you are dead.

". . . Two is better than one—especially with insurance policies"

DOUBLE
COVERAGE 9

One of the things that I will always be **grateful** to my parents for is their insistence that I get medical insurance coverage once my condition was diagnosed. After all, I was a typically irresponsible 22 year-old with no real job— playing in a band barely paid any money, let alone a benefits package.

So, I signed up with King County Blue Shield. My mom would make the payments for me each month just in case I was on the road or forgot—and I'd send her the $18 per month for my coverage. $18 per month for health insurance! Remember, this was 1979—I have recently paid as much as $700 per month.

Why? Well, with my pre-existing condition I simply canNOT afford to let my coverage lapse—doing so would be insane—I'd never be able to either afford new insurance coverage or the bills associated with a major surgery.

As expensive as my health insurance is, it's nowhere near the close to half a zillion dollars I've incurred in bills.

Which brings me to this amazing example of just another reason why health insurance is so very expensive.

In 1992 I was hired for a full time teaching position at a junior college. Even though this position included a full benefits package, with a group health plan, I still maintained my own private plan.

Well, with atypical shortsightedness I one day approached the president of the college, who also happened to be a CPA, and ran the following brilliant idea past him.

"Hey Rich, I said, wanna save the college some money?" "Go on," he replied, his ears perking up. "Well, since I already have my own personal health insurance I don't need double coverage. Why doesn't the college pay my premium for me and not include me in their group package? We'll both save money", I proudly proclaimed. "Sorry, Bob, no can do, it's against the contract rules", he said. Oh well, it was worth a try.

Sometimes it's better NOT to get what you want. Here's why.

In 1994, when I had my first surgery, private plans, like my Blue Shield, did NOT coordinate benefits with group plans (like my college coverage).

What did that mean?

Both insurances paid the full amount allowed, approximately 80% of the bill, after deductibles, etc. Two insurances each paying 80% equals 160%, so all of the doctors, the hospital, the technicians, etc. were paid 60% too much.

Guess where that extra 60% went? (dramatic pause) To myself. Yep, me. So, how does something like that happen?

Simple . . . group and individual plans did not coordinate and recognize each other, and, because of their policies and whatever laws, I couldn't have returned the money even if I'd wanted to. And you might find this incredibly stupid, but I actually contacted the insurance company at one point to find out where to send these checks back to—they told me that they couldn't take them back, that the money was mine to keep.

So check this out:

I made the mistake of sharing that information with some friends. And you know what? A couple of them were actually jealous, saying I was so lucky, or, that I was ripping off the insurance companies.

Lucky? I wouldn't go thru open-heart surgery if you paid me $33 million dollars, let alone $33,000—and I didn't rip anybody off, that was the system.

I wonder how many MILLIONS of dollars have gone to waste because of various health insurance plans that didn't recognize each other. Just another fine example of bureaucratic brilliance, at our expense.

Yeah sure, I made some money, but like I said . . .

In November of 1994, just weeks before my second surgery, and another "lucky" payday, Washington state laws were changed and benefits were finally coordinated. Darn it, no more lucky paydays.

As long as I'm on the topic of health insurance, this brief story is for anybody who works the front desk or answers phones for a doctor.

I was getting a second opinion and called a doctor who I had never been to before. A lady answered the phone with "Doctor's office." "Yes, hi, my name is Bob and I'd like to schedule an appointment." "Who's your provider?" was her reply.

Who's your provider? Why not just ask if you have any money, whether or not you can pay the doctor, better yet, just cut to the chase and find out if you're a deadbeat . . . I mean that's basically the implication of the question, isn't it?

When someone calls a doctor, chances are that they're sick. With a cardiologist, they probably have some type of heart condition. In my case, I had just been cast adrift by my own doctor, was facing a another possible surgery and was feeling severely overwhelmed. And the first thing they ask me is "Do you have any money?" I was livid.

I understand and agree with their need to get paid. But how about some basic dignity and compassion? How about answering the phone with "How can we help you?" That would feel and sound so much better, especially during a difficult time.

Well, as I'm prone to do, I told the lady exactly what you just read, and in no uncertain terms.

Do you know what she did? She apologized and THANKED me for pointing that out to her, and told me that she would change right away. And furthermore, she asked if I could call her right back so that I could hear the difference. I did. It sounded better. It felt better. I was still in a world of hurt, but for just a moment I felt like I wasn't so alone, that somebody cared.

We ended up having a nice chat and when I went for my appointment, I met her and she said that that small change had made HER feel better, too.

 Healthy Heart Tip: Compared to hospital food, healthy food is YUMMY!

" . . . Ask not Why Me—but ask: Why NOT me . . . —JFK"

HOW COUNT THIS *HAPPEN?* 10

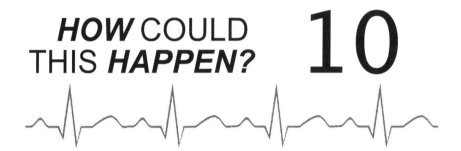

"Dear Terry, I saw Bob Sluys in the office today and have reviewed his echocardiogram. There is definitely a step up in velocity across his right ventricular outflow track distal to the valve. In addition, on physical examination he has a loud systolic ejection murmur. I have to do a little checking around with some of my peers who have been doing the Ross Procedure . . . blah blah, blah blah . . . Bob, although quite disappointed, understands the problem and I believe has confidence enough to solve the problem. Thank you very much for your support. I am sorry the results are not perfect, but we need to figure out the problem so that we can prevent it in future patients."
Best regards, Edward D. Verrier.

That was from a letter dated December 2, 1994 from Dr. Edward "The Big Toe Puller" Verrier to Dr. Block.

Wait a minute, what's going on here?

I had only had my long-awaited heart surgery a few months ago. I'd been told that I would be an excellent candidate for the Ross Procedure, that I could expect perfect results. I had even been told that I was beautiful and had my big toe pulled. This can't be happening . . . this wasn't supposed to happen!

Well, it was and it did.

Something had gone wrong, but what? Was it something I had done? Or not done? Did I attempt to come back too soon? Was it my diet? Did the doctor screw up? I replayed the past few months over and over in my mind.

At first my recovery had seemed slow—although I'm certain it was progressing by normal standards. I can get pretty energized and I'll admit that I was champing at the bit. I was pumped up, I had a new lease on life—after all, I had prepared for this for over 15 years and now I was fixed! I would finally be able to do what I wanted. No more worrying if that dark cloud of coronary restrictions was going to once again rain on my parade—the clouds had parted and the sun had broken through —and this was in Seattle!

I had followed the verbal prescription that is the norm for heart surgery patients: I didn't drive for a few weeks, didn't do any heavy lifting, took it easy on the caffeine and wine, and tried to keep my stress as low as I could.

After a couple of weeks I had started to write the new show for the college. I slowly started exercising, well I call it that but it mainly consisted of just walking, then slow jogging, lots of stretching, shoot a few hoops here and there. The whole process is slow—sometimes you feel like you're not making progress, but eventually I was doing pretty well. You just try to slip back into your routine; work, family and recreation.

Around the Fourth of July, my friends John and April came up from California—they were considering a move to the Seattle area. Angi and I invited them to stay with us.

One night I had just gone to bed and as I lay there I noticed that my pulse seemed irregular. It's strange—insignificant things that we never pay much attention to all of a sudden become hugely magnified when they impact our lives.

Your heart rate, post surgery, can take weeks to settle down to its baseline norm . . . and as per the norm, mine slowly came down. Well, I kept feeling my neck (the easiest place for me to get my pulse), and sure enough, it was skipping all over the place. SHIT! Something must've gone terribly wrong . . . and I was scared shitless.

I asked Angi if she could also feel the skipping—she could.

Damn.

I was going to die, or at least have to have a re-operation. I couldn't believe it. I had no choice but to go to the hospital, so John took me down to Good Samaritan hospital and, after the usual battery of tests I was diagnosed with a reaction to a cold medicine that I had been taking. It caused my heart's electrical circuits to go whacky and resulted in the chambers not moving in sync.

The next time that you pop a Dimatapp, Dristan or Contact read the instructions: do not take if you're a heart patient.

What a sense of relief! At least I wasn't facing another (insert coughing sound) surgery.

Right now I feel the need to vent. To offend, perhaps, but what I'm about to say comes from the core of my soul and depths of my passion.

I HATED going through open heart surgery. It sucks. It hurts. It messes with you mentally, physically, emotionally and spiritually, IN A BIG WAY. And, I don't give a rip if some of you old codgers out there who have been through it think (or say, because I've heard you) "Hell, it wasn't so bad, just a few days and I was good as new. Why, I didn't feel a thing." Screw you. You're lying or you're in denial. Or, you had better drugs than me, and, if so, now I'm REALLY pissed off!

The first couple of months had gone very well. But, by the end of September I began to notice that I was getting tired more quickly. I didn't seem to have the stamina that I had or expected. I didn't feel right. I mentioned it to family and friends and was told by some that "You worry too much Bob, you're fine", or "get over it, get on with your life" oh . . . okey dokey!

Unsolicited medical advice usually always comes from people who haven't been there. Now I know that people might feel helpless, that they mean well and want to help—I get it. But shut the **** up!

So—instead of preaching I'll just toss in this inspirational quote: *"Before you criticize someone, you should **walk a mile** in **their** shoes. That way when you criticize them, you are a mile away from them and **you have** their **shoes**."* —Jack Handy

By the middle of November, I knew that something wasn't right and I made an appointment with Dr. Block. He examined me and somberly told me that the pulmonary valve was emitting a loud and harsh murmur. After some other tests, he said the words that deep down I already knew, that I would need another procedure.

I was shocked, stunned. How could this happen? What had happened? Why did it happen? What do I do? I had put all of my emotional eggs in that first basket. Would I have enough Mojo for another surgery?

I was crushed. I felt cheated, ripped-off. But, by who? God? Dr. Verrier? Dr. Block? Myself? It wasn't fair . . . oh yeah, I don't do "fair", sorry, I forgot.

Dr. Block was obviously disappointed but at the same time didn't have any answers. He suggested rejection or even "technical error" —wait a minute . . . could it be possible that Dr. Verrier had screwed up?

I met with Dr. Verrier and he seemed more concerned about his track record as a surgeon, stating: "this kind of thing doesn't happen to him". He was right—it didn't happen to him, it was happening to me! And, as was par for the course, he did all, or most of the talking. Told me that he would fix it. Done deal. That he was the best. Blah, blah, blah . . .

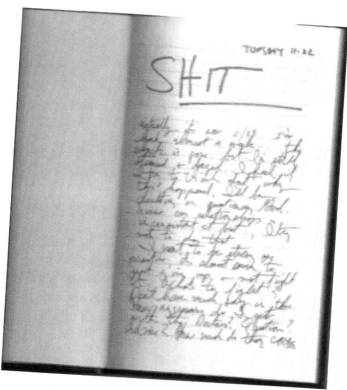

Angi gave me a journal—I wrote in it for about a week . . . as you can see, I don't hold back . . .

I was still in such shock that I basically just said OK and we set a date of December 19. 1994 for the surgery. I figured that that would give me almost two weeks of the Christmas break to recuperate and I hopefully wouldn't have to miss any class.

Let me say this: I was a complete **IDIOT** for wanting to return to work just 15 days after a second open heart surgery. But I did. After all, I was committed to my students and my program.

Committed. Yeah, I should've been committed all right.

The next day was Thanksgiving. The big family gathering was at my brother Pete's house. I was severely depressed, and I'm sure that it wasn't easy on my family, either. My brother-in-law Ed greeted me with "Hey, I heard that you liked it so much you're going back for more" If that was an attempt to cheer me up, strike three, baby. I remember taking a long, long nap later that day.

Later, a few of us were playing Trivial Pursuit. Being the bottomless pit of useless knowledge that I am, I ran off about seven or eight answers in a row. I then had to hear someone complain that I was the luckiest person he'd ever seen. Lucky was the last thing that I was feeling.

On Sunday night, December 18, 1994, we had our family Christmas celebration. The next morning I had to be up at 4:30 for round number two. I did my best to be up, hell, this was the second holiday in a month that I had affected, and understandably, it wasn't the most joyous occasion. The toughest moment came when my parents gave us their gifts. My dad had spent months editing custom videos for each of us kids. Culled from home movies and stills from photo albums, they were each mini life-in-reviews. They even had soundtracks. It was a wonderful gift, straight from their hearts. As he handed out these tapes, my dad said that this was exceptionally difficult, with what I was facing in the morning.

We all then watched the tape. It was everything I could do to keep from crying, and I'm sure that others fought the tears as well. Thanks again, Mom and Dad for a very special gift.

4:30 a.m. arrived much too early. Once again, I took a "double shower" washing twice with a special soap. And, as before, I wasn't allowed any food or water. You don't realize how much you enjoy that morning latte until you can't have one.

It was dark and the roads were deserted as we drove to the hospital. The butterflies were getting warmed up a little sooner this time, it seemed.

We went to the same cubicle and I put on the same gown. Took the same little pill so that I could relax. (Those pills don't work, by the way). I got on the same gurney, and wouldn't you know it, there was Robert rushing out of the same elevator after another all-night drive from Salem.

This was just too weird. It was like the movie Ground Hog Day—and I was Bill Murray. We said our goodbyes . . . I was wheeled into the same pre-op room, with the same colorful birds and trees on the ceiling.

The anesthesiologist started the same I.V. lines, and, of course, it just wouldn't be a proper deja vu homecoming without the same grinning chest shaver.

SECRET HIDDEN BONUS CHAPTER!

We've all heard various versions of the positive affirmation phrase "living in the moment"—or for you linguists, "Carpe Diem-*Seize The Day!*"

Now, not to be a Debbie Downer, but at first glance this seems to be a wonderful concept—especially when **things are going well**!

However—as with everything in life there are exceptions, and the one thing you DON'T want to do is to *live in the moment* during the heart surgery process. The first 24 hours are the toughest, and then you develop a routine, get used to things and before you know it, you're home in your LazyBoy™ recliner munching on popcorn and watching a *Golden Girls* marathon. Estelle Getty? Grrrrrr....

So—let's talk about those first 24 hours.

Yes, you're on morphine and everything is being done to make you comfortable. But the plain truth is you've been invaded. Assaulted. Cracked open—in a traumatic way.

Sorry.

The first 24 hours is the time to breathe deeply and focus on good and pleasant things. Things that bring joy or comfort. Family. Faith—a good cabernet for under $10.
Cuz there's another great phrase that works even better here —"This, too, shall pass."

During my first recovery I had no idea what to expect. And even though it sucked that I ended up undergoing a total of four heart and one hip replacement procedures, it was easier for me to deal with once I knew that in just a few hours or days I would feel 1,000 times better—and I would focus on that, NOT live in the moment.

Look—you're ultimately gonna be just fine! You'll feel better than before your surgery . . . heck, you might even end up writing a best selling book, although, I really don't need the competition.

And if that doesn't work; remember—there's always *Carpe Morphine!*

Family portrait time! Circa late 1980's . . .
Back row L-R: John, Jan, Pete, "The Klink's", Irene, Ed, Me.
Front: Jason, Cara, Oma, Monique and Ryan.

". . . Is not adhering to the Hippocratic Oath hypocritical? Keep reading and find out!! . . ."

PENETRATING QUESTIONS 11

I was slowly starting to **regain my senses**. After the harrowing experience with the Shish-ka-BOB . . . oops; sorry, that was *last* surgery.

I awoke to the same leering grins and demented calliope music as before. This time around, being that it was Christmas, there was no room at the inn, so I had to stay in the CCU all night.

It wasn't exactly a Christmas party—fluorescent light bulbs hung overhead, shining right into my eyes. No sleep. An old man was right next to me on (or is it in) an iron lung. Every few seconds a very loud whoosh followed by an even louder click, throughout the entire night. I got very little sleep—actually, I wouldn't consider any time spent in a hospital bed as sleeping.

I threw up my steak and green beans, right onto my incision.

The nurse was sarcastic and short—impatient, I mean—not vertically challenged..

The next few days were pure hell. I hurt. They took blood until I had none left to give. Nurse Ratched had a cold, and she seemed intent on giving it to me, glaring at me whenever she could, and spraying me with a well placed sneeze or cough. Oh, and whenever injecting something into the catheter in my hand, she would push that plunger as quickly as the medication would go in, just to heighten and enhance the pleasure that the burning and stinging sensation would bring. Falalalalaaaa la la la laaa, indeed.

Once, I called a nurse to be taken for a walk, and one and a half hours later a first year Pakistani exchange candy-striper promptly arrived, speaking some sort of gibberish that neither one of us seemed to understand.

Attaboy, University of Friggin' Washington, "A National Leader In Health Care"

Bob, you're so angry. No I'm not, and be quiet before I smack you.

Something was up. For one thing, Verrier "The Toe" was nowhere to be found. I guess that I was no longer "beautiful, beautiful" . . . although, I thought that I was still quite handsome. And the nursing care? It was atrocious.

My friend Phil visited on the second day, and I was feeling pretty lousy. He arrived at the same time as my overcooked "mystery meat" and hard roll worthy of use as a spring training batting practice projectile. Phil is a minister, and although we don't really keep in touch, I appreciated his visit.

That brings up an important point. Very few people, hardly any, in fact, asked anything more than "how are you feeling? Or, they pipe in a cheery (bad grammar notwithstanding) "you're doing good." I have yet to have someone ask what my emotions were, my deepest thoughts, my fears, what things felt like and so on. Maybe that's one of the reasons why I'm writing this book and recording a CD—so that you CAN know . . . actually, no, you can't know until you've been there . . . but at least this might give you a better understanding of what it's like.

For all of my family and friends who were there: I know and appreciate the fact that it must have been very difficult for you, too. I also understand that it's almost impossible to know what to say or do. I can't thank you enough for being there for me.

Well, the sooner I was out of there, the better. And on December 23rd, I was.

There was Pat and the borrowed minivan. And, what did I have for lunch? Fettuccini and a glass of wine, of course, after all, old habits die hard!

Once again, Angi outdid herself in the home healthcare department. By the way, Angi and I started our relationship on the day that I scheduled my first surgery and she endured all three (at the time) of them. Our entire relationship encompassed my health problems, and unfortunately, she was second on the list of priorities. It was a matter of survival.

One night Angi and I were watching a brand new TV show. It was called Chicago Hope; it was a drama that took place in a hospital. This particular episode was about an elderly Rabbi whose heart was failing. In fact, he needed a complete transplant. And of course he went into the O.R. for the procedure.

The surgeons removed his heart and instructed the nurse (who happened to be a close personal friend of the Rabbi) to get the donor heart—which she promptly dropped. As the heart landed, it slid, at which time it was accidentally kicked, coming to a rest underneath a cabinet. As this Hollywood moment was unraveling, so were Angi and I. That whole scene cut just a little bit too close to my situation. As farfetched as it was perhaps, could something like that really happen?

Now let's roll up our sleeves for some good stuff.

You typically see your surgeon for a follow-up visit about two weeks after your discharge, and so, I went to see Verrier.

After some awkward chitchat and an exam, Verrier asked me "How was your care?" I thought that to be a strange question, but I answered, " Well, since you're asking, it was awful." I then told him about the nurses, and so on.

Get this: "Well, you know why you received poor care, don't you?" he said. "No, actually I don't know why that is", I replied. "Well, it's because of what you said." 'What I said?" "Yeah, in the operating room. As you were coming out of your anesthetic, you asked "Did he get it right this time?" Verrier quickly added, " That didn't bother me, of course, (yeah right) because I knew that you were still under, but my staff was very much offended."

I couldn't believe what I was hearing.

I was blown away. The staff of the Professor and Chief at a major hospital gets bent outta shape because of something a patient says without the patient even knowing that they said it. And then, diverting the blame to the patient. Remember; the "get it right technical error seed" had been planted by Dr. Block.

At this time I must warn you that I feel another soapbox moment coming on.

To be able to perform open heart surgery takes supreme ego and confidence (ya gotta move like Jagger), and I wouldn't want anything less from my surgeon. But that ego, even coming from his staff should NEVER be allowed to interfere with the healing process of the patient whose life you just saved. What could be more hypocritical and unacceptable? And it's just plain wrong. Shame on you, University of Washington.

Well, at least that explained my horrific care: Pissed off nurses. Hey! That sounds like a new reality show!

In a letter to Dr. Block dated January 6, 1995, Verrier writes " ... *Mr. Sluys definitely is somewhat hostile about the whole procedure and the fact that he required re-operation. I have spent considerable time with him in the hospital and yesterday in the office reassuring him that this was a possibility and what we felt was his best treatment options. I think I have assured him, but I believe he will continue to ask penetrating questions with somewhat of a chip on his shoulder.*

He continues with "*I obviously wish that every operation always went perfectly, but clearly we are in a learning phase for this particular operation . . . "*

That's right, Verrier—penetrating questions that MAYBE I should have asked before you started slicing and dicing.

And why should penetrating questions threaten you . . . unless . . . maybe, you have something to hide? And, are you attempting to "alert" Dr. Block?

Let's ask a few penetrating questions right now.

#1: Why was the first operation unsuccessful, and what did you find, rejection or technical error?

#2: Since you were putting a foreign substance in my body (the donor valve) why didn't you put me on anti-rejection medication the first time?

#3: If it was rejection on my part, why didn't you give me anti-rejection medication following this second surgery?

#4: Since you didn't give me anti-rejection medication in spite of your "rejection" diagnosis, didn't you in fact commit malpractice by exposing me to the extremely high risk of yet another surgery?

#4: Why didn't the Northwest Tissue Center ever receive the "rejected" valve that you took out so that they could perform a biopsy, as per standard procedure, and, and why were their and mine requests for the valve ignored by you?

#5: If you really are in a learning phase, as you claim, regarding the Ross Procedure, who specifically did you consult with before just so brazenly cutting me open?

#6: Did any of the doctors suggest the possibility of rejection, and the course to take if that indeed was the finding?

#7: Your hospital consent form, which I signed, states: "the risks, including the risk of bleeding, infection, myocardial infarction, stroke, respiratory or renal failure, the need for future surgery, heart block, and death." Where does it mention "rejection"?

There—are those enough penetrating questions for you?

Here's something else that raises a huge red flag. A week after my first surgery in June of 1994, Verrier performed the exact same operation on a young woman in her mid twenties. It was his 8th Ross Procedure. Her result also went bad and she was re-operated on about a week after my re-operation. I don't know her outcome, but I hope that she, too, asked lots of "penetrating questions."

In fact, if there's anything to have been gained from my experience it's this: ASK LOTS OF **PENETRATING QUESTIONS.**

It's your body! It's your life! Make it your duty, your obligation, your responsibility to find out everything that you can: about the doctor. The procedure. The hospital. Medications. Billing. Anything that you may have concerns over. Everything. Down to whether you get orange or lime jello. There are no stupid questions. Not asking questions is stupid.

Ask them directly. Get referrals. Go online. And if you happen to piss somebody off, tough darts. Find another doctor.

Do it.

Chillin' with my cat Pebbles. Resting and napping have become favorite things to do.

Healthy Heart Fact: Each year, over 300,000 Americans die of smoking-related heart disease.

"_. . . If only there had been Craigslist in 1996, our hero wouldn't have had to do what you're about to read. Fasten your seat belts . . ._"

THE *SEARCH* 12

It felt like I'd been there a thousand times before. Flat on my back in one of Dr. Block's examination rooms. He was hunched over me, stethoscope in hand, with a stern look of determined concentration on his face. I tried not to look at his eyes cuz that's where the diagnosis would first appear. He deftly moved his stethoscope around my chest, sometimes pausing at certain places—move it a little bit— pause, go back to a previous spot and so on. But the eyes would have the answer. They had before.

Sure enough, a few moments later the look of concentration became one of concern and maybe even one of frustration. But there it was, nevertheless. As he ended his dance of the stethoscope and motioned for me to sit up, I knew. I had known for weeks.

"Well Bob, he started . . . there's definitely a much louder, increased murmur at the pulmonary valve. We'll need to get another echo, of course. It's not an emergency, but it looks like you'll need to have another surgery."

Was I surprised? No—shocked? Not really, not anymore . . . It was more of a . . . a numbness, a deflation that settled into my entire body.

"I really don't know what more to say or do," continued Dr. Block. "It's a very difficult problem and I don't have a solution. I'm obviously in over my head." Hmm, a difficult problem . . . no solution . . . in over his head . . . Damn. I really WAS in big trouble.

Dr. Block then said something that really pissed me off. "If you'd like, I'll call around the country and run it by some other doctors, see if they have any ideas. Why don't you give me a couple of weeks or so . . ." A couple of weeks or so?

NO, GET ON THE PHONE RIGHT NOW AND FIND SOME ANSWERS.

A couple of weeks or so? We've been together over 16 years, through two catheterizations, one of which almost killed me, and two open heart surgeries with a third now looming on the horizon and you'll get around to it in a couple of weeks or so? You BASTARD. That was exactly what I thought and how I felt.

*This was in the fall of 1995—I no longer harbor that anger or have any feelings of ill will . . . but at that time, I was not a happy camper.

I went to go see Dr. Verrier at the University of Washington, and as luck would have it, I had lost my voice. Lucky for him, cuz I had prepared the Mother Of All Diatribes; instead, I just sat there miserably trying to croak out an occasional question, all while he dispensed such gems as "sometimes life isn't fair . . . you gotta play the hand that you're dealt . . . I know how you must feel . . . why didn't he just shut up and stitch some needlepoint samplers of his quaint homilies.

Is it just me, or is "I know how you must feel" some sort of standard response for the clueless and insensitive? After continuing on and on about how this kind of thing never happens to him, he wished me luck. I needed more than luck.

Needless to say Verrier was obviously out of the picture. There would be no more pulling of my big toe.

In fact, a few weeks later Verrier wrote to Dr. Block: *"I certainly believe that Bob and you would probably be more comfortable if somebody else attempted to put this homograft in since I have now given it two shots, both of which I thought were technically perfect, but both of which caused re-stenosis."*

The previous 8 or 9 months had been the same slow, gradual process of recovery as before. There were occasional victories and setbacks, but nothing of consequence. I must admit that I was harboring a lot of anger, but at whom I wasn't sure. Verrier? Dr. Block? God? Myself?

And now, and I would once again have to try to get myself psyched up.

I waited until the beginning of November before telling my class. They were quite shocked and very attentive as I spent a couple of hours telling them my health history and explaining what was going to happen. I made a commitment to them promising to do my best, and told them that I expected the same in return. I also asked for their understanding if and when I had down days and needed them to motivate and energize themselves instead of relying on me.

It wasn't easy, it never is, but then, why should it be? How can anything that challenges us in life, from illness and disease to life itself be easy? But don't we often respond, when faced by an unpleasant task or situation that's "too hard", by burying our heads in the sand by way of booze, drugs, spending money, overeating, et all. If you're getting tired of hearing this, too bad, because I'm not even anywhere close to tiring of this subject. Besides, not only am I writing this, but I too am going to read it as well.

Now back to my search. First of all, I didn't wait for Dr. Block to make his calls. I got out the phone book, (this was pre-internet) called around, got referrals—I did whatever it took to try and find someone to help me.

By the way, I originally produced an abridged audio version of this book onto compact disc in early January 2000 (updated in 2012 after yet another surgery—keep reading!). I sent some copies out to family, friends, Dr. Block, Verrier and people familiar with my situation.

Within a few days Dr. Block responded with two messages left on my phone machine. Although he admitted that he found it to be "95-98%" accurate and even entertaining, he highly resented my use of his name, especially if I were to produce the CD and publish my book for commercial gain.

He also found it "narcissistic and self-absorbed." Hahaha! Folks: this is classic and priceless—who better to recognize narcissism and self-absorption than a doctor? BUT— *he was right.* To be able to dig back, relive events whilst in 24/7/365 survival mode requires being COMPLETELY self-absorbed. Trust me—you don't want to find out for yourself . . . as for the narcissism, well, all I can say is that thank God for spell check . . .

Oh; and, he took exception to my account of this very chapter, stating that he, too, helped find surgeons to visit during my search.

That's OK, we're all entitled, but I stand by my account. Finally, the good doctor severed our 20 year relationship.

ANY open heart surgery is a matter of life and death. They knock you out, crack your chest, stop your heart and take it apart—hopefully without a slip of the scalpel, all while a machine pumps your blood and keeps it oxygenated for you.

Then, you need to be revived without having suffered a stroke, serious bleeding or an infection.

No matter how strong you are or how good the doctor is, it's always life threatening. Sure, it might be routine for the medical professionals, but to me, it was anything but. Like the bumper sticker says: shit happens. No matter how much I wanted to believe my own words when I told people "ah, it'll be a piece of cake."

By the end of February I had scheduled a weeklong cross-country trip in search of a surgeon. Talk about your logistical nightmare. Airline reservations and flight connections, surgeons and their schedules, motels, rent-a-cars, groupies—you name it. It was a zoo, I felt like I was booking a rock 'n roll tour.

On Monday, February 26 1996 I caught a flight from Seattle to St. Louis.

The search was on, the game was afoot, you could say.

As we flew high over the frozen tundra I felt a certain chill inside. This was it. I couldn't afford to make a mistake. How many more times could my body endure being cracked open and disassembled? Forget my body—what about my mind? Like Indiana Jones in that Holy Grail movie, I had to choose wisely. I had to find someone who would save my life.

I arrived in St. Louis, spent the night at Tom Bodette's place (yep, the light was on) and Tuesday morning at 11 a.m. I had my first meeting. His name was Dr. Kouchukous, and he was a world-renowned heart surgeon. I had prepared packets for each of the doctors that I would be seeing and I handed one to him. It contained echo study videos, charts, previous operative reports, the whole shebang. I had also created a list of questions that I would ask each doctor as I conducted my search.

Let me backtrack a little bit. A couple of months earlier, in November, I had called Dr. Block's office asking for photocopies of my complete file. Well, that was a ton of paperwork, over 16 years' worth. Doctors don't seem real thrilled about releasing any paperwork to their patients. Why? Are they hiding something? Jeez, you probably think that I'm paranoid. Well, I'm not. And why are you asking, uh?

Since Dr. Block had told me that I might be better off with another doctor, I needed my file for my upcoming trip. So one day I received a call from his nurse. She told me that my file was ready and that I could pick it up at 1pm. When I arrived, they wouldn't give it to me. It wasn't ready. Or they couldn't find it. Or the nurse in charge was at lunch. Or . . . crap, I had to get back to work. The head office lady started arguing with me telling me I would just have to wait. I'm already hypersensitive, facing yet another surgery, I've have been abandoned by this doctor and now his staff is stressing me out.

Just then Dr. Block appeared and told me to quit arguing with his nurse. He didn't even bother to find out was the problem was. I was furious. What the hell were medical professionals doing causing a heart patient stress? I should've known better, because it had happened before. It seemed to be all about them.

I must admit that I've always liked Dr. Block. Whenever I'd fly up from Los Angeles for my annual checkups we'd talk hoops, show biz; looking back it seemed that he was interested in me as more than just a patient, and in spite of everything, I believe that he was.

He was also pretty straight forward, almost to the point of seeming un-compassionate. He even acknowledged to me that his bedside manner wasn't exactly his strong suit. Bingo.

But in all fairness to any doctor, can we really expect them to be anything more than . . . just a doctor? Hell, they've seen us naked, listened to our complaints, probed our bodies, maybe even opened us up, took us apart and put us back together. Exactly how much closer can we expect them to get? I'm not suggesting that they take home with them the lives and problems of every patient that they see, of course not.

If you're a doctor who perchance stumbled upon this writing, we know that medicine becomes routine for most of you, that's probably to be expected. I'm just asking that you try to remember that it's NOT routine to the patient; in fact we're pretty much scared to death.

Let's check back in with Dr. Kouchukous. He examined me and looked at my file. He didn't appear too enthused about my situation (I'm so damn demanding, aren't I?) and I didn't get that gut feeling I was looking for. I thanked him for his time and continued on my journey.

Next stop—Oklahoma City, you know, where the wind comes sweeping down the plain and some crazy nutjob blows up the federal building murdering a bunch of children. Boy, can I pick 'em or what!

After renting a car and checking into yet another Motel 6, I arose early and got ready for my meeting with Dr. Ronald Elkins. Dr. Elkins was a world-class surgeon with lots of experience performing the Ross Procedure. His staff was outstanding. I immediately became infatuated with one of them . . . we'll call her Sherry. This meeting went very well. Dr Elkins was calm and yet had a dynamic, commanding presence. He reminded me of Christopher Plummer circa *The Sound Of Music*.

He explained my options as well as a very detailed version of what he would do to ensure the best possible outcome. Briefly, here's what he told me:

He would use a cryopreserved donor valve, as before. But he called it an "ALT" valve, one that has been treated so that it didn't have as many living cells in it, thereby hopefully eliminating the possibility of rejection. He did caution that because the valve wasn't "as alive", there could be no guarantee that it would last me another 30 or 40 years. They would also have to put me on a very potent dosage of anti-rejection medication, in the form of Prednisone. More details on that lovely experience later on in the show.

Well, at this point I didn't have a whole lot of choices. I was sold.

I said my goodbyes, and hopped a plane to Houston. I already had this visit scheduled and thought that getting a second opinion of Dr. Elkins' plan might be wise.

Dr. D. Mott of the world famous Texas Heart Institute saw me around noon. He examined my file, listened to my heart and drawled, "Boy, you're in a heap o' trouble."

Criminy, I felt like I was making a guest appearance on the Dukes Of Hazard. He went on to explain that he NEVER performed the Ross procedure—after all, why take a perfectly good valve, and mess with it?

NOW you tell me! And, he said, your chances are slim. He then informed me that he didn't think he could be of any help. Thank you Dr. Mott, oh, and could you please say hi to Daisy for me?

Well, Dr. Elkins, like the song goes, it's just you and me. I guess I'll see you in June.

I then had the pleasure of taking a direct flight back to Seattle, with short stops in Dallas, Albuquerque, Phoenix, Oakland and just about every other town on the west coast. There's nothing like 6 or 7 hours on a plane to contemplate all of the things I had heard the past few days. And in spite of flying on an airline that only served peanuts (yeah you know who you are), that was a lot to digest. Now that was funny!

Speaking of funny, for some people the toughest decision they will ever face is whether to drive the Beemer or the Lexus to lunch with the girls at either Spago or Puck's, and, should they go shopping afterwards at the Beverly Center or Rodeo Drive? Stop it, it's . . . it's . . . all so confusing.

On the Phoenix to Seattle portion of the trip, the plane was almost empty (but there were plenty o' peanuts). I was sitting in a section where the two rows of seats face each other. Just me, and a beautiful bleached blond lady. We started chatting. She was a national sales rep for a (of course) drug company. She was flying around the country to meet with various doctors. Me, too!, I told her!

She asked about my trip and I gave her a brief outline of my story. We ended up having a great conversation. It was the perfect medicine—I got a lot of stuff of my chest and she was sympathetic, always a good combination. She was also married to a PGA tour golfer. I almost asked her if she preferred Spago's or Pucks . . .

I must be honest about something. In many ways this trip was exciting. I was flying around the country like some rock star, doing one-night concerts. I was taking my future, my very life into my own hands. I was making choices and decisions. I felt like I was doing something, fighting back. Against what, if anything, I don't know. But it was a very vibrant experience. In spite of the bleak circumstances, I felt very much alive.

I finally got home at about midnight and set my alarm for 6 a.m. I had to . . . go back to the airport! Only this time, I was taking my class on a field trip to . . . Las Vegas. No Partridge Family school bus to the local museum of tree pruning for my class, nosireebob, we were off to sin city.

When I arrived at the airport, my students were all very anxious to find out about my trip, but, I was bound and determined not to let it affect me, or them.

We had a blast. It was the perfect antidote. I even hit four deuces on a quarter machine and left three days later up about $700. Which I put in my wallet. Which fell out of my pocket. Which I discovered was missing after the plane landed. Which was discovered in the nick of time by my friend J.J.—he rushed back to the plane—my days of O.J. Simpsoning it thru an airport were on hold at the time. I was running more like Homer Simpson.

And, now, once again, it was just a waiting game.

The two Sherry's-they did a great job in helping coordinate the logistics for my surgery.

". . . Wanna know the secret to leaving Vegas with a small fortune? — arrive with a large one."

GO DOWN
GAMBLIN'

13

June 20, 1996. The date was set. My third and, hopefully, last surgery. Well, like they say, 3rd time's a charm. I've always wondered who the "they" is that come up with those quaint little sayings. Remember, there's also three strikes and you're out. To be honest, I wasn't quite sure how much I had left in the gas tank. The first time I used up quite a bit with the 15 years of anticipation and anxiety, the surgery and the recovery.

Then the second time was such a challenge due to the let down, the holiday season, the stress on family and friends, the horrific care and attitude by the medical "professionals" and again the process of recovery.

Normally if life, seem to get easier the more we do them. We develop a routine, gain some experience, and learn from our mistakes.

I'm here to tell you, heart surgeries (probably every surgery for that matter), are a bitch every time. You're NEVER quite ready.

It was Memorial Day weekend just a scant few weeks 'till D-Day, and my brother Pete called. In just a few hours he was leaving for his annual softball tournament in Reno. His wife Joy couldn't make it and he asked if I wanted to get away for a few days. "You bet", I enthusiastically replied.

After all, gambling seemed to be all I'd been doing lately, with doctors, choosing procedures, and so on. Besides, it was a chance to go visit my money.

Here's a quick tutorial on gaming destinations for all of you gambling neophytes. Those millions of bright lights and flashy neon signs? Paid for by losers. Those "free" buffets? Ditto. Four days in Reno is about five days too long. You budget yourself two to three hundred bucks, accepting that you'll lose and go have a good time. And if by some chance you win, well, . . . don't hold your breath. Oh—here's a little nugget that I love to share: "Wanna know how to leave Las Vegas with a small fortune? Arrive with a large one!"

Ok, enough positive talk. We get to Reno, Pete plays some ball, I sit in the sun; life's not too bad. That night in one of the casinos we discover a new table game called Let It Ride. If you're REAL lucky you can win big, but most of your hands are losers. After just a few minutes Pete gets a 4 of a kind and wins over $300 on a three-dollar bet. Me? Not a thing. And that was just the beginning of a brutal weekend. I couldn't get a winning hand to save my life, and Pete did very well.

I was pissed off!!!!! Not at Pete, but at . . . fate, If there is such a thing. I needed a victory. I was the one having another heart surgery. Why couldn't I have a few moments of pleasure instead of feeling like a loser? Damn, I sound whiny.

And now for a public service announcement courtesy of . . . Me.

Pay close attention to these words. Words of experience. If you're in a difficult situation, whatever it might be, don't gamble. Don't drink. Don't put yourself in a position to fail. You're guaranteed to hurt yourself and those around you. Some giant hand is not going to reach down and rescue your poor self-pitying butt. Luckily, I survived—after all; I had a surgery to go to!

A couple of weeks later, just a few days before leaving for Oklahoma City, the band I was in had a gig at the Java Jump, an all-ages club in Tacoma. Everybody I invited showed up. People that normally wouldn't be caught dead in a club, people that hated the type of music we played; it didn't matter, they were all there.

You wanna know what I thought? That it was a mercy gig. They had come to pay their last respects, just in case I bit the big one the following week. That's what we do, isn't it? Someone's in trouble, we make a quick appearance, feel better about ourselves, and then when things are going well again, we're nowhere to be found. Human nature, I guess.

I used to kid with my brother Pete that the only time he ever comes to my house is after I've had a surgery. It's true. I live less than a half hour away. And, he's not the only one. Since I plan on not having more surgeries, I did the only logical thing— I sold my house and moved in with him and his family!

Back to the gig—to add insult to injury, the sound man was incompetent, the sound system blew up during a song, we were way too loud . . . it was a truly painful experience all the way around.

Tuesday, June 18, 1996: T-minus 45 hours. SeaTac airport. My folks and I were in the check-in line and Angi arrived to see me off. She brought me some flowers. She had wanted to come to Oklahoma but wasn't able to, and instead would be house sitting and caring for Pebbles, my cat. My brothers Pete and John would come out the next day, as would Robert from Oregon. My sister would make it out two days later. I felt nervous but assured Angi with another one of my famous "piece of cake's" — yeah, right.

During the flight I was quiet and sullen. My mom asked me at one point, "what's wrong, where's the jokes, why aren't you talking"—here's my Homer Simpson-esque response—doh.

Tuesday, June 19, noon: T-minus 18 hours. (Damn, this thing's starting to read like a Tom Clancy novel.)

I checked into the hospital for a battery of tests and questions, the normal pre-op procedure. I was to spend the night in the hospital, but I asked if I could leave for a few hours so that I could host my 3rd "Last Supper."

It probably sounds morbid but it was a chance to have fun with my family and friends, to reassure them that my spirits were OK, to enjoy a good meal and a couple glasses of wine, and, to REALLY be a hero of course, by paying for it all. At 9 p.m. we headed back to the hospital, and, another round of goodbyes.

My family is not an "I Love You" kind of people, but I felt what everyone was feeling. I was feeling it, too.

Robert insisted on staying in my room with me on the foldout chair. By the way, please be advised that you can ask for a family member to stay in the room with you. If you want to, that is. Unless they snore—then it's a bad idea . . .

When we got to my room, there was a knock on the door and two strangers in black coats came in. It was Joliet Jake and Elwood Blues. Just kidding, actually they were two Mormons

Last Annual Grand Reopening

 INFO

WHEN: THURSDAY, JUNE 20 1996 - 7am

WHERE TO CALL: (405) 271-4633 ask for Bob Sluys

WHERE TO WRITE: To Bob in care of Dr. Ron Elkins
920 Stanton Young Blvd. #4SP250
Oklahoma City, OK. 73104

RETURN TO SEATTLE : UAL #1419 From Denver
Arrive 4:15pm Saturday, June 29

OTHER INFO: Comfort Inn (Oklahoma base for family/friends)
4017 NW 39th Expwy. 800-628-5011

THANKS FOR YOUR PRAYERS AND SUPPORT !

An info/contact flyer I made for family/friends.

sent by a colleague of mine at the college. We chatted and I
appreciated the gesture. But I wasn't ready for my last rites
quite yet!

At 9:30 pm, a nurse came in and said that she needed to
take us to cardio intensive care for some instruction on things

to come. We both thought that to be rather odd, since they didn't do that at the University of Washington the previous two times. Hmmm, there seemed to be a LOT that they didn't do at the University of Washington.

Our visit was eye opening and disturbing. The nurse explained all of the tubes and lines I would have in me. That my hands would be tied so that I wouldn't try to rip the tube out of my throat. That I wouldn't be able to talk. On and On.

I found myself getting anxious and nervous as all of my old memories resurfaced, memories that had been slowly fading away where now all of a sudden bigger than life all over again, right in front of my eyes. There was no turning back. As much of a bummer that little tour was, I'd still rather know than be kept in the dark. I've said it before and I'll say it again: for me, **the hardest part of any of this is the unknown.** The fear comes from the scenarios we create. I'm not saying it's a day at the beach, but knowing what's to come really does lessen the anxiety.

Robert and I got back to my room at about 10 o'clock, and surprisingly, I went to sleep right away and slept quite soundly. Somehow I felt a certain peace. I had done all that I could, and it was now it was out of my hands and in God's.

 Heart **Surgery Recovery Tip: You may resume sexual activity in about two weeks—but only with your spouse— the doctors don't want you getting too excited.**

. . . "I have no clever insight or witty saying for this chapter"

OKLAHOMA'S
A OKAY!

14

I was slowly starting to regain my senses. After the
harrowing experience with the shish–ka–BOB . . .
darn it, I keep having the same Deja Vu!

For you kids considering a career in medicine or perhaps
fans of Grey's Anatomy, here's the verbatim transcription of my
operative report as dictated by Dr. Elkins.

*The patient was brought to the operating room where after the
induction of satisfactory of general anesthesia multiple IV's, a radial
artery line, a foley catheter and a central venus pressure line were
inserted. The patient also had a trans esophageal electrocardiogram
probe and also had a swan-ganz introducer which was used for
apherisis of platelet rich plasma.*

*After positioning, the patient was prepped with alcohol and draped
with a sterile drape.*

*A median sternotomy was carried out with the excision of his previous
scar. After opening the sternum, the adhesions, which were quite
dense were carefully lysed to provide access to his right atrium. Both*

the superior vena cava and the junction of the inferior vena cava in the right atrium and to provide access to the ascending aorta.

A double purse string suture was placed in the ascending aorta.

Two separate purse strings, one in the superior vena cava and one in the junction of the inferior vena cava and the right atrium were placed for vena cava access.

The patient was heparinized, cannulated and attached to cardiopulmonary bypass, and bypass was instituted without difficulty. The patient was cooled to 32 degrees just to slow his heart rate while we operated. During the cooling phase, the adhesions were taken down until we could adequately visualize his pulmonary homograft.

His pulmonary homograft, which had significant obstruction in the distal portion of the homograft actually wound up being a relatively normal pulmonary homograft with normal leaflet function.

There was severe desmoplastic reaction around the homograft and around the autograft and it appears that the autograft had been wrapped in pericardium. The homograft that had been placed had been attached to a segment of pulmonary homograft from a previous operation and this distal segment was a part that was markedly narrowed.

These areas were totally excised and after the excision a 25 millimeter pulmonary homograft serial number 3871398 was placed. This is an alt homograft which has reduced viability and it was implanted with a running 4.0 proline suture proximally and a similar type suture distally. After establishing continuity of the right ventricular outflow track the patient was rewarmed.On reaching 37 degrees bypass was discontinued without difficulty. The patient came off bypass quite satisfactorily, protamine was administered, hemostasis was obtained a single chest tube was inserted and the chest was closed in layers in the usual fashion.

Sponge and needle count was correct at the end of the procedure.

As my friend Pat like to say after we've successfully landed after a flight in his home-built experimental airplane . . . "cheated death one more time!" I'd made it! I'd cheated death again!

And once again I was recovering from yet another surgery.

My stay in Oklahoma was fantastic. The doctors and staff were outstanding. Oh yeah, there were a few challenges— Robert had become an expert on the spirometer and nagged me to death over it. I understand that he was also a maniac driving go-carts, running little kids off the track . . . I love that man!

I was brought sausage and biscuits & gravy for breakfast— job security, remember? But, for the most part, the food wasn't too bad.

I also finally got my own u-operate personal morphine dispenser. Let me tell you this about morphine: the pain doesn't really go away—you just don't care . . . like I mentioned previously—it's smooth, it's warm and it's powerful.

After a few days, I was put on the anti-rejection drug prednisone.

One of the many things that Prednisone does is to shut down your immune system—in other words, it tricks your body into accepting a foreign object, like in my case, a donor heart valve.

At first it was wonderful—I was euphoric, so happy to be alive that I couldn't sleep! I felt that God had finally rewarded me for the price I had paid all of those years with a clean bill of health—it was too good to be true!

Alas, as with all things that appear to be too good to be true, it wasn't; and my euphoria didn't seem to come from God, either.

It was the prednisone.

". . . Need Prison? Try some Prednisone instead! —*anagram courtesy of my close friend www.scrabbleguy.com"

PREDNISONE 15

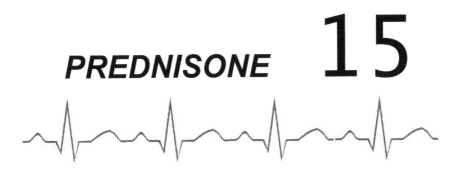

Five days post-surgery **I checked out** of the hospital. Dr. Elkins had requested that I stay in town for a few extra days so that he could do a follow up.

My folks, my sister Irene and I visited the Oklahoma City bomb site memorial; we went to a western art museum, went shopping at the mall—I saw a movie. I sat by the pool in the cool breeze of the night sharing a glass of wine with my folks—THAT'S not recovering from a third open heart surgery—that's a vacation! Remember, this was in part a courtesy of my new friend Mr. Prednisone.

The morning of my trip back to Seattle I had my follow up visit with Dr. Elkins. While waiting to see him (waiting to see a doctor? — yes, some things will never change), his staff played me a video of him performing an identical open heart surgery.

I cried like a baby—if you've never seen such a video— words can't describe it. I felt such thankfulness and compassion for this man who had given me another chance.

Interestingly enough, I later found out that Dr. Elkins had undergone open heart surgery himself some years later. I had no way of knowing that I would also see him again 15 years later.

Clowning around in front of the hospital entrance. Amazing - just 5 days after open heart surgery. Stunning. Not my clowning, but what God, medicine, and humanity can accomplish. I'm still in awe.

At this point I'm feeling the need to do a little preaching — about praying and miracles.

Now I'm not going to go into the philosophical depths of the power of prayer—but I'd be willing to bet that almost everybody faced with surgery reaches out and says some type of prayer— or their loved ones do . . . but, are they answered? The easy answer is Yes! No! Or, maybe . . .

Since no one has ever figured this out definitively and since it's really a matter of individual faith I can only offer my experience.

Now, according to the American Heart Association God allows oh, about one million folks to join him each year as a result of heart related issues—does this mean that He didn't answer their prayers!? Myself, well, I'm still here, so, did God answer my prayers and perform a miracle?

I believe that He did—but indirectly and in His own way.

Watching that video of Dr. Elkins performing such a delicate and intricate procedure made it all so clear: God saved me through Dr. Elkins.

It's simple—here's how.

God created man, and God gave man the ability to learn and grow, and through the centuries man evolved and developed skills and cures and open heart surgical procedures!

It's sort of a spiritual 'the ankle is connected to the leg bone."

So by creating us, God DID perform his miracle, albeit thousands of years later and through Dr. Elkins.

At least, that what makes sense to me, and it's what I've chosen to believe.

After receiving a (relatively) clean bill of health from Dr. Elkins—and he received my heartfelt (sorry, couldn't resist) profuse thanks & appreciation we headed back to the Pacific Northwest.

We touched down in Seattle at about 7 pm. I was tanned, — looking sharp and feeling fantastic—prednisone.

I got off the plane and was greeted by . . . Batman . . . Sonny & Cher . . . the cast from Grease—Madonna? . . . some strange looking guy in a tank top—oh, that was my brother . . . I was overwhelmed!

A welcoming committee of my students, family, friends and all in costume from our latest show! Well, this called for a celebration!

Sure enough, everybody came over to my house for a big party—I called Pat & Mette-Lisa . . . they rushed over—this time in their own car!

The wine flowed and there were stories and laughter and the showing of my scar and breathing contests with my spirometer, which, of course I won—it's all in the technique, baby —and I had more experience than I could ever want!

The next month was sheer joy—I couldn't sleep—I didn't need to! Prednisone.

I was finally cured, and I was gonna sue Dr. Verrier for about 8 billion dollars—prednisone.

Prednisone.

A typical dosage is 5 to 10 milligrams per day—sometimes up to 60 milligrams; I was on 80 milligrams per day. Dr. Elkins had pointed out that this was not an exact science. Due to an insurance company requirement, I was on that dosage for a month, instead of the prescribed two weeks.

SAY WHAT?

In 1996, at this time, my insurance company required that you submit labels from your prescription in order to get reimbursed for your prescriptions purchased out of state. This was before the whole internet/computer system they have now. And so, I took the labels off of my bottles—the labels with the DOSAGE AND INSTRUCTIONS!

When I started running low, I called Dr. Elkin's office in Oklahoma City for a refill, and was told that I should already have been weaning off!

DAMN!

I was immediately reduced to 40 milligrams per day and that night, I woke up with such excruciating pain in my knees that I cried as I crawled from my bed to the phone—I had to get to a hospital.

The pain was so bad that I was unable to raise my body to reach the phone and eventually, I must've passed out. I woke up hours later—still on the floor, the pain having subsided. And so, over the next few weeks I was gradually weened and it was pure hell. I had apparently become addicted.

Prednisone can become a nasty nasty drug.

Some side effects, all of which I seemed to have experienced include psychosis, acne, weight gain, bruising, severe cramping, nausea, vertigo, headaches infection, depression, behavioral changes and osteoporosis.

Prednisone also reduces the blood flow to your major joints, which can cause the cartilage to die, resulting in the possibility of joint replacement! Oh boy! Something else to look forward to!

I didn't know what it was or what to do . . . my right hip had become very painful and I ended up seeing an orthopedist . . . after examining the MRI he said that I had bone on bone and would some day need hip replacement surgery.

Damn again! (In fact, I had my right hip replaced in 2006.)

It was during this time that my moods and personality changed by the second. I was constantly sick—several close friends and family members bailed on me.

Whilst struggling with my recovery my sister Irene made some sarcastic comment to me that I took as insulting and embarrassing. I wrote her a scathing letter a day or so later, one that I first ran by all of my other family members and one that they agreed with, too. So on went that stamp and off went that letter.

That letter resulted in my being estranged from her as well as my brother in-law and niece and nephew.
They all fired off their letter in response—and it wasn't pretty.

About a year later Irene sent me a card with a sincere apology and we agreed to meet for lunch where I too offered my sincerest apologies

I'm so thankful that she took the first step because I'm not sure that I would've. Irene could be very high maintenance (as could I) and I just didn't have it in me to deal with at that time. Well, about a year after that Irene was diagnosed with a very rare and ultimately fatal Pick's Disease. I'll remember Irene in another chapter.

I'm glad that she had the courage to contact me—I can't imagine how I'd feel if we hadn't reconciled. And what ever that feeling might be, I know it's nothing to the fate that awaited her.

I had just survived three heart surgeries due to a birth defect, and now my sister contracts a disease that is thought to be genetic? I can't even begin to comprehend how my parents must be feeling. The guilt over having created deformed babies must be tremendous—I know it was because my mom said so.

But know this—I have never ever blamed them for my misfortune nor will I. And I'll say it again mom and dad—it just happened—things happen in life.

Next on the agenda? Sue the pants off of Verrier!
During this time, August of 1996, I had consulted a malpractice attorney. I spoke several times to his Paralegal and told her the whole story. She was incredibly interested, involved and positive—this is exactly the type of situation we represent,

she told me, and I think you've got an excellent case! I was pumped!

Well, we met in his Mt. Rainier-view downtown Seattle penthouse offices. I was armed with a veritable armored car containing all of my medical file—reports, videos, letters—everything.

After a lengthy meeting with him and his staff, he announced that although I had obviously been damaged and that at least one of my surgeries had probably been unnecessary it would be very difficult to win my case.

Self portrait—in the throes of a very common post surgery occurance . . . feeling angry & depressed. Van Gogh I'm not!

Say what?

I thought that I had a slam dunk! What about the lack of informed consent? The lack of medicine to combat potential rejection, the missing valve from the first surgery? This was gross negligence! What am I missing here?

Here's what he went on to say.

Take a look at yourself. You look great! Tan, fit, healthy . . . no missing limbs, no squirting blood. No jury's gonna find in your favor! They'll just think that you're an ungrateful punk trying to ruin the career of a faithful dedicated servant. Dr. Elkins won't testify against Dr. Verrier, plus, the University of Washington is a state institution making Dr. Verrier a state employee therefore, his attorney will be the Attorney General for the state of Washington, and they'll have unlimited resources, which you don't have.

You simply have . . . no . . . chance.

And so I sat there and let it all sink in. I had no fight left in me. I thanked him for his time and slowly walked out of the room.

As I drove home I thought, OK, maybe I'm not gonna get what I deserve but hey! I'm still alive and that's all that really matters, and from here on out, things can only get better! 30 minutes later I turned onto my street. I was having JJ paint my house that day and I could hardly wait to see it. I pulled into my driveway, and like a giant slap in the face was greeted by my freshly painted pink home!

I was now living in a Baskin and Robbins.

Cone, anyone?

The kids in the 'hood will LOVE me, I despaired.   Somehow the color on the tiny little swatch from which I made my choice didn't quite translate to the walls of my house.

Maybe it *wasn't* gonna get better . . .

SECRET HIDDEN BONUS CHAPTER #2:
A REUNION . . . OF SORTS

In the fall of 2007 I went to a local P.F. Changs in the Seattle area. I was going to meet my friend Joey for a bite. It was a typical cold and rainy Friday night and as I walked into the restaurant the place was packed. I was a bit early and so I ventured into the bar area. As I looked around for a place to sit I saw him.

There was no mistaking it—even though it had been over a decade I immediately knew him. In an instant I was overcome with all the emotions I had experienced since that first diagnosis in 1978.

I became nervous, angry, scared, confused—and yet I couldn't take my eyes off of him.

Since the place was packed, he too was looking for a place to sit. I turned away for an instant and when I looked back he was gone.

Where did he go? I HAD to talk him—this might be my only chance, and now he had disappeared. I rushed out to the entrance and looked out into the dark pouring rain. After just a few seconds I spotted him and I headed for the door. As I started to meet him, he came back towards the entrance. I stopped and waited.

Once he was back inside I took a deep breath and with my pulse racing at a million miles an hour I approached him.

"I know who you are," I said, from behind.

He slowly turned, looked at me and replied "I don't think so . . . that's not possible."

"Yes it is, I replied—you're Dr. Verrier. I'm Bob Sluys . . . remember me?"

"Yes, I'm Ed Verrier—I remember you."

As I gained my voice and confidence my feelings subsided, and, for the next few minutes we chatted—I told him about my third surgery in Oklahoma City. He told me that he had stopped performing the Ross Procedure—in part due to the poor result that I had achieved.

Our chat was civil, yet we both were obviously uncomfortable. He went on to mention that I could expect no more than maybe 15 years on my original valve replacement.

He would be off by two years.

And that was it.

I walked away and when I had gone about 10 feet I turned around and headed back towards him. Our business was unfinished.

He saw my approach and appeared apprehensive. I stuck out my hand and said "even though I was very angry with you, deep down, I know that you did your best—and I have no hard feelings."

He shook my hand and replied that "he had done his best and that he was glad to see that I was doing well."

We wished each other the best and once again I walked away.

A little while later Joey showed up and as the crowd had gone into the restaurant for their meals we found a seat at the bar. Joey, obviously knowing my heart history listened intently as I, still shaking, recounted what had just transpired.

As we talked I noticed that Dr. Verrier was also seated at the other end of the bar, with whom looked to be his wife and maybe his kids. We caught each other's eye and he raised his wine glass—as did I.

I teared up when I told Joey—and later, when I called my folks to tell them, I did as well.

Now—what are the odds of us meeting like that so many years later? Astronomical, at the very least. But I'd faced astronomical odds before—and would again.

I truly believe that it was more than a random meeting. I firmly believe that running into Dr. Verrier was divine intervention. It had to be.

I needed forgiveness and some closure—and it seemed like Dr. Verrier did as well.

It felt good.

There I am on the right, playing my bass just a few weeks after surgery #3—higher than a kite on Prednisone . . . I wasn't trying to show off the fresh scar as much as I was sweating my butt off!

 Healthy Heart Hint: Diabetes can be controlled through changing eating habits, exercise programs and avoiding Walmart, where apparently it's contagious.

. . . "Poor, poor, poor me—poor poor pitiful me"

SHUT UP, WARREN ZEVON 16

I was sitting at my computer putting the finishing touches on the script for my audio book CD that I was to produce. It was the end of December, 1999, and as I glanced out the window, I said to myself "looks like we'll have a white Christmas this year." Only the white would be fog, not snow.

Fog—that seemed to describe exactly how I'd felt the past three and a half years since my last heart surgery. It was funny, in many ways those three and a half years had been much tougher and more challenging than the 17 years prior and during.

The emotional ups and downs, the uncertainty. The anticipation of achieving a positive result, followed by the deep disappointment when things went south. The anaphylactic shock episode. The wear and tear on my body being sawed open three times, taken apart and put back together. The countless injections of countless medications. The neurological damage caused by the cardiopulmonary bypass—a condition identified and known as "Pumphead"

The Prednisone. And on and on and on. Damn, I think I'm going to need a Kleenex—but only because I have a cold.

In many ways, the aftermath and side effects of the past 20 years had actually created their own new disease, and I couldn't tell which was worse.

My chest and arms have been constantly stiff and sore, to this day. My right hip is very painful, especially after exercising. My feet cramp severely, limiting my ability to jog and run. The fingers in both hands routinely go numb— which makes playing the bass guitar very tricky. I nick myself shaving and I bleed for an hour, thanks to my daily aspirin. And I still can't cough or sneeze without grabbing my chest to keep the ensuing pain in check.

An MRI revealed that I had suffered a stroke, probably during my last surgery, and it also discovered a brain deformity called Arnold-Chiari malformation. Gee, another birth defect.

The college eliminated my program and I lost my job. I loved the program and considered it an honor to get paid for sharing my knowledge and experiences with my students. Not having fathered my own children, it was a way for me to hopefully have a positive impact on the lives of young people. But, it was a very stressful job and it's probably just as well that I no longer teach.

Finally, I'll probably never quite be out of the woods. Remember, there's no guarantee that my aortic autograft or the pulmonary homograft will provide permanent fixes . . . there's certainly a real chance that I'll be facing further operations down the road.

Had enough? There's more:

Late one night in October I was sitting at my computer and I just started to type, putting my thoughts into words. I have no idea why I was doing that, maybe I needed closure, to put a period on that part of my life. I don't type very well or very fast, but I sat there and after a couple of hours this is what I came up with:

October 14, 1999 – midnight

I'm excited for the future, because the past year has seemed even more challenging than my recent health issues. This is a woe-is-me list designed to help me focus on better things ahead. Here goes, in no particular order of importance, my year in review—damn, I just realized that there's two and a half months to go.

1. My sister Irene is diagnosed with the rare and fatal "Pick's Disease". She is now at Western State Hospital.

2. My Grandma suffered a major stroke at age 90 and is withered and ready to die. She can't talk or eat.

3. My friend and former band-mate Denver is in the last stages of Lou Gehrig's disease, is invalid, and was recently kicked out of his home by his loving wife, "who isn't dealing with this very well." Oh—she's not. I see.

4. My modest monthly disability payment was stopped with no warning and a feeble explanation.

5. My brand new mountain bike was stolen after I forgot to bring it inside. $400 right down the drain.

6. My best friend Robert is dealing with some very challenging health and mental problems.

7. My body hurts.

8. My former student and roommate left to go on the road and he owes me over $1000 on back rent.

9. My hair loss has been dramatic and noticeable. Well, at least to me.

10. I went on a date with Becky (who wasn't into

muscular, model-looking poseurs–perfect!!) A date. One.

11. I asked Susie (who is lonely and lives nearby) if she'd like to go to the Puyallup Fair. She said she'd rather have a root canal.

12. Brittany, a pleasant girl I met recently, invited me over, and after three hours of playing Yahtzee told me that she's normally very talkative and interesting.

13. Oh, almost forgot, "Summergirls", a band I spent 15 months and $19,000 (my entire savings) on, broke up due to pregnancy, alcoholism (no, not me), legal actions and . . . apathy. Mine.

14. I was forced to sue a former performer in small claims court for not returning items belonging to me . . . and lost to a femi-nazi judge who did everything but consider the evidence—when she allowed me to present it.

15. I produced a video for my former Tae Kwon Do school—pretty much at my cost, WAY under their budget – and spent three and a half months trying to collect my money. When they finally paid me, they shorted me $130 – and got pissed off at me when I pursued it. You're welcome, glad to be of service.

16. I went to Reno with J.J. for the annual Scrabble tournament. Nine years ago, I was smart. I won $750. Now, I've gotten really dumb. Got spanked. Not a lot of words with the letters " uuiiavo" in them.

17. Oh, I also lost nearly $1000 gambling—trying to keep up with J.J.—who didn't do much better. I no longer gamble, at least not with games of chance

18. My brother John invited my friend Robert and me to Alaska for a once in a lifetime guided fishing trip. His roommate, also an Alaska Airlines pilot was to take us in his private float plane to an isolated lake for some trophy fishing. One problem—his roomie was up all night giving it to his girlfriend and told us that he was going back to bed 'cause he

didn't get any sleep. So Robert and I spent two days driving around like Laurel and Hardy—and got shutout. No fish. None. Zilch. Zippo. Nada. No bites. Impossible. Never, in the history of fishing in Alaska had somebody not caught a fish. Thanks, roomie, hope you had a good time.

19. Trying to sell my house (since August, in a hot market). No offers. Lookers. Anybody. It really is a nice house.

20. Auditioned for, and got the gig, a 70's Disco show group in Las Vegas. Only two nights per week and GREAT money. I'd commute. Be a big time rock star. It fell thru. Show Biz sucks.

21. Summergirls had a gig where the sound-man screwed up in too many ways to mention. I stopped payment on the check, BECAUSE HE HADN'T DONE THE JOB. He sued me. Used a lawyer, for whom his wife works. I consulted a lawyer, but defended myself. Lost the case. His lawyer had case law that was a year newer than the case law MY lawyer gave me. I owe nearly $1000 to some slacker who almost cost me the gig, and HE gets rewarded. I love our legal system.

22. New math for the over 40 crowd. For each hair that you lose from your head, you grow three NEW hairs on your back. How come this doesn't apply to women? Actually, that's probably a good thing.

23. One day, my car started running rough. I took it in to a mechanic who told me, after an hour of computer diagnosis and getting really greasy and grimy, that I had a thrown rod (which is not to be confused with a blown seal, a condition quite common amongst lower class Alaskan prostitutes.) *joke courtesy of John Sluys.

That happened on a Friday, so I spent all weekend trying to find an affordable junked motor—the estimate for the repair being $3,500! On Monday morning I arrived (driving my rent-a-car) to have my Blazer towed. The mechanic offered me $1,500 for my junked car. (Blue book is $7,800) I declined his offer and took my Blazer to another mechanic for a second opinion. Two minutes later, his "opinion" discovered a loose spark plug wire —which he reattached, for free, my Blazer ran great, and I saved $3,500. Damn, I wish I had done some other "second opinion" gathering about 5 years ago . . . . .

Well folks, I could go on, but it's late, I'm tired, and I'm sure that you also have a story about your past year that I'm certain could easily rival or even top this one. Like I said, I'm excited about the future, 'cause, well . . .

That was what came out of my soul and brain that late night in October. Ouch, pretty damn pathetic. I mean your old buddy Bob. Me. Those girls? Hell, I wouldn't have gone out with me, either. Some of those things can just happen, but once I put it down on paper, purged myself and was able to read and digest it, it became fairly obvious that I was either putting myself in situations to fail or that I at least had some sort of self-generated sub-conscience crash and burn vibe accompanying me.

Putting all of those thoughts and feelings down on paper was an amazingly positive and therapeutic process. I'd never done anything like that before in my life! It was cleansing; an emotional, mental and spiritual enema. It certainly didn't solve any of my problems but the process itself, the focus and discipline it required really helped me to start seeking closure.

These were all challenges, yes, and I didn't enjoy them. But I submit to you that it will take much, much more than all of that to break me or bring me down. Defeats suck. We all want victories. After all, only losers like losing. Maybe I'm all out of victories. Used 'em up, like timeouts in basketball. We'll see.

Besides, I'd have nothing to bitch about.

P.S. Oops, I almost forgot all the positives!

Uh . . . er . . . a . . . um . . . well, ah, . . . there's . . . uh . . . mmm . . .

Like all good legal documents (or mediocre memoirs), this chapter has some amendments. Didn't think you were gonna get off that easy, did you?

October 15: Got a call from an agency who had hired me to play bass for three gigs in December, including New Year's Eve in Las Vegas for $1000. They cancelled me due to concerns about Y2K flight delays.

October 19, 1:30 am: After working for hours trying to solve a mixing problem with my computer, I broke down in tears yelling "ENOUGH, I'VE HAD ENOUGH". A few hours later at 5:30 am I awoke with the worst imaginable chest pains– I called JJ and told him I was driving myself to the ER — spent eight hours there, with every possible test performed. The diagnosis? My heart was fine, but I'd suffered a stress-induced meltdown.

October 26: Received word that my grandma had passed away. I immediately flew to Holland for the funeral. Although she'll be greatly missed, there was a sense of relief that her suffering had ended. Nevertheless, it was not the easiest thing to experience.

November 7: Received word that my good friend Larry had suffered a heart attack and was being prepped for emergency open heart surgery in Albuquerque. I flew down right away and spent two days with his family. He did quite well and the prognosis is good.

Today, Nov. 11: Got an email from the director of the cruise ship for which I had interviewed for the Musical Director position, telling me that they had decided on a pianist instead of a bassist.

I sent copies of my "list" to a few family and friends. They all thought that it was FUNNY! That I should write a book! Maybe it was entertaining, but my year had been anything but fun.

In Bar Harbour, Maine with my best friend Robert. We traveled to the east coast for some "world-class" fishing, as Robert promised. As per usual, we caught NOTHING! Circa 1997—one year after round #3.

 Healthy Heart Tip: Reduce stress by NOT going fishing with Robert!

"... Some things will never be explained nor understood ..."

IRENE **17**

I'm gonna stray off of my loosely choreographed chronological path and **pay my respects to my sister Irene**. Irene was the first born—February of 1955. She was about 18 months older than me.

Was.

Irene succumbed to Pick's disease in August of 2004—a few days before my parent's 50th wedding anniversary.
Here's what Wikipedia tells us about it:

Pick's disease is a rare neurodegenerative disease that causes progressive destruction of nerve cells in the brain. Symptoms include loss of speech (aphasia) and dementia. While some of the symptoms can initially be alleviated, the disease progresses and patients often die within two to ten years. A defining characteristic of the disease is build-up of tau proteins in neurons, accumulating into silver-staining, spherical aggregations known as "Pick bodies".

Basically, Irene had contracted an incredibly rare affliction that would ultimately prove fatal. Irene first started exhibiting symptoms in the late 90's. Long story short, she ended up in various institutions and homes, slowly degenerating into a state of being on a feeding tube and such.

Initially, nobody—doctors included—had any idea of what was causing her "dementia"-type symptoms. Remember, the internet was in it's infancy—there just wasn't anywhere to go for information. And we tried—I spent many hours online trying to find answers. Not that the doctors weren't, but you feel helpless and want to try and contribute any way that you can.

One thing that DID enter our minds was the fact that my aortic stenosis is congenital, and now my sister has a what appeared to be congenital disease—what was going on here?

I had read a study that indicated that my condition, the aortic stenosis, was caused by environmental influences—and my mom was raised in a German occupied World War II Holland. Could this have played a part? Been the cause?

She had been between ages roughly 4 and 9 during the occupation, and I'd heard more than one story about hunger and other difficult conditions. Add to that the pollution caused by the tanks, machinery, bombs and chemicals everywhere—

well, it certainly wouldn't be a stretch to think that this had played a part in our birth defects.

We'll probably never know. Still . . .

I did do some googling on Pick's disease recently (2012)and from what I read, apparently it's not considered to be handed down.

My folks were basically "recovered" from dealing with my situation when Irene's came up. Brutal. I know it had a great impact on her husband Ed and her kids Jason and Monique. And I once again bring up the fact that pain or suffering or whatever is not lived and experienced on a curve.

Your stubbed toe should not be minimized by comparison to someone's cancer. They are both a challenge and painful and . . . what I'm saying is that we are all different and we all need to respect each other's situation with empathy, at worst and love and compassion at best.

Irene and myself in Den Haag, Holland-circa 1960

There will ALWAYS be someone better off, worse off, richer, poorer, stronger, weaker—you get the idea. I HATE when the martyrs minimize their pain with "Well, this isn't as bad as _____'s cancer or heart disease" perhaps not! But that doesn't make it any less painful for you.

I was financially ruined by the real estate meltdown years later. Since misery loves company it DOES make it a little bit easier to handle knowing that millions of others suffered the same fate, but that doesn't make me any less poor!

I could nor would ever compare my experience with Irene's. And the fact is, she died. I'm still here.

Irene was cremated and the following summer we all gathered at Sunrise Park on Mt. Rainier, where her ashes were scattered. It was . . . I dunno, I don't want to dishonor it—it was just a strange thing. Not easy.

Irene, being a Dutch female got in her last lick, though! As Ed and my dad were scattering her ashes a gust of wind came up and I distinctly remember getting some ashes in my face. It made me smile on the inside—her spirit lives on!

The entire Sluys clan on Mt. Rainier visiting Irene's final resting place—August 2012.

. . . "Idle hands are the Devil's playground."

MEAN*WHILE* ... 18

My **third heart** surgery was in June of 1996. In the years that followed it I first went through my recovery period. Here's the deal that never seems to get talked about— recovery from anything is a full meal deal, meaning that there's the physical aspect; usually involving a level of therapy and such. Additionally and just as importantly are the mental, emotional and spiritual components as well. Throw in family, friends, job and you now have a full blown operation—no pun intended. It's an all-consuming beast with a life of it's own.

Sufficed to say, I had more than one challenge and adventure during this time. The details will be outlined in my memoirs—look for them at fine booksellers everywhere!

Seriously, in the late 90's I moved from my house in the sticks to an apartment in Kent. I started a group called Summergirls—we played dance hits from the 70's, 80's and 90's—it was fun to be onstage playing my bass and it was also a lot of work, which I didn't mind.

I got in good enough shape to play hoops 3-4 times per week at the local athletic club. Just being on the court was a tremendous blessing and gift. I also played a little bit of indoor soccer—I was in my early 40's but still was able to run and compete.

I helped my brother Pete coach his son's basketball team. The internet was coming into it's own and I got involved for a short time with a startup MLM—multi level marketing—company.

In short, I kept pretty busy.

In early 2000 I played a few shows with a Vegas-based Elton John impersonator—more on him in yet another book called *Gay Drama Queen Divas and Their Bands I've Played In*.

I even went to mainland China for a 5 week tour. By the end of 2000 I was feeling the need to do something different. Part of the reason was the same as always—the gray and gloom of the Seattle weather. The other reason was the gray and gloom of the Seattle weather.

My right hip had started barking and I thought that a drier climate would help. Plus, my folks had retired to there and maybe I could do some gigging.

I moved to Vegas in March of 2001 and in the next few years played music and sold real estate. I did some investing as well.

April, 2004 saw me spending 4 days in the hospital—I had been experiencing shortness of breath and saw a cardiologist.

TAKE NOTE!!!!!!!!

If you EVER experience shortness of breath or chest pains, immediately go to the ER. They will not turn you away, and it might save your life!

The doctor told me that he wanted to do some tests, including a procedure involving nuclear medicine. He said that getting things scheduled, etc, could take some time: OR, he "recommended" that I . . . just check into the ER, complaining of chest pains and I can get all of this done right away!

I did, and after four days of various tests I was given a clean bill of health. I remember my girlfriend Stephanie and my friends Mike and Linda stopping by in the evening, usually having smuggled in a bottle of wine.

In 2005 I traveled to Costa Rica to look into developing land, and a few weeks later found myself in South Africa producing a video for a faith-based AIDS orphanage.

Next thing you know, I was back in the Northwest, buying a house for the AIDS foundation and getting involved at the emerging rockstar Mars Hill church, led by Mark Driscoll. I did some real estate as well and ultimately ended up back down in Vegas.

Man—I truly am the poster child of homelessness!

In 2006 I finally had my hip replaced. I didn't get the best result and it's still sore to this day. Before the operation I had to once again see my cardiologist to show the orthopedic surgeon that my heart could endure the stress of a hip replacement.

Then, the housing bubble and financial meltdown hit, and I got nailed. Wiped out. I was ruined financially. Talk about stress. Truth be told, without my faith and past experiences in dealing with life-threatening issues I'm not sure exactly how I would've made it through this.

By 2009 I was bouncing around couch surfing between various family and friends. In fact, the last time I'd slept in my own bed—ha, "own bed"—I don't even OWN my own bed . . . was in August of 2004.

As I write this in late 2012, I'm essentially homeless. But—no time to wallow! It's almost time to go have another surgery!

Tongue-in-cheek comparison . . . no lightning bolts, please . . .

Jesus was homeless. Me, too!
Jesus had no possessions, just a posse. I have no posse.
Jesus worked with wood. I worked in a band with a drummer named Woody.
Jesus was a carpenter. My favorite singer is Karen Carpenter.
John and Paul wrote about Jesus. George and Ringo wrote about Yellow Submarines and Tax Men. OK—that was a stretch . . .
Jesus' right-hand man was Peter. My brother Peter is left-handed.
Jesus' mother's name was Mary. Mine, too, although Jesus' father's name was not Theo—BUT, Theology IS the study of God and it contains "Theo"—am I good?
Jesus hangs out with Angels. My girlfriend was Angela.
Jesus turns water into wine. I turn wine into what will eventually become water.
Folks—are you starting to see a . . . well, it IS uncanny . . .

 Healthy Heart Fact: That wet stuff pouring down your face when you workout is called sweat!

". . . At some point, you start losing track."

IT'S **NOT** JUST LIKE **RIDING** A BICYCLE

19

Towards the end of the summer of 2011 I was starting to notice some huffing and puffing—even when I was just out for a walk. I had seen my cardiologist a year earlier, and he had said to come back in a year. However, at those times I was not working and penniless. I didn't pay him and so I figured I couldn't go back. My bill had even been sent to collections.

I had maintained my health insurance, but at over $700 per month AND a $2,000 deductible I just couldn't swing it. I contacted my provider and ended up lowering my premium but raising my deductible—it was now $5,000.

By the beginning of November I called my cardiologist and explained my situation. They said that I could come in for an exam if I paid $100 cash. Whew—ok, I was certainly thankful for that.

I scheduled an appointment with Dr. Ward, saw him and he said that before making a final determination he wanted to perform a TEE—a transesophageal echocardiogram. Basically, I'd be prepped, sedated and then a ultra-sound probe would be

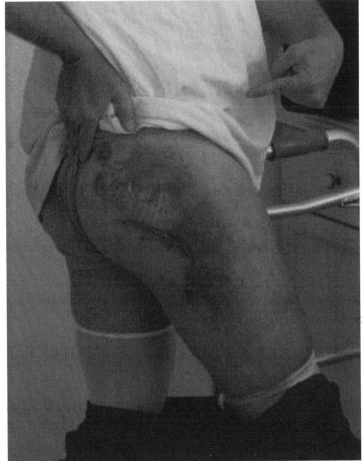

2006—My hip replacement! A good way to take your mind off of heart surgery—dig the sexy silk stockings! Grrrr....

threaded down my esophagus for a better look at my heart valve. I'd be swallowing a camera. Sweet.

A few days later my dad and I drove to the hospital for the 6 am procedure. When I woke up a little while later the doctor told me what he had already told my dad—my aortic valve that had originally been harvested from myself 17 years earlier was finished. Done.

I was facing an unprecedented 4th open heart surgery.

I was 55 years old.

Deep down, I had already known that some day I would likely need another surgery. I'd had frank discussions with amongst others, my minister and he even suggested that if it came to that maybe it was just God telling me to come home. Perhaps—there were times that I was just beat down and done. Finished. I simply didn't care any more. Would this be one of those times?

Dr. Ward also needed a treadmill test and so we scheduled one. I'd had probably a dozen or so—they were fairly routine. You could also die during one. My friend Teresa's father I believe, had suffered a coronary during his in Taiwan a few years earlier. You just never know.

However, me being Bob Sluys, you DO know what's coming next, right?

Of course you do. Would you really expect me to have any experience in life without something going wrong? Heck, I even check the toilet bowl for pythons or alligators before I sit down to do my business—not that I'm paranoid!

I arrived for my treadmill and they prepped me—shaved parts of my chest for the sticky thingees that take about a month to completely wash off and I jumped on ready to go.

Every three minutes they would increase the speed and incline. At around the 8 minute mark, I was cruising along, huffing and puffing but able to keep pace. All of a sudden, a buzzer went off—and so did I.

I'd been watching the monitor that displayed my heart rate and other stuff when boom, my heart rate spiked up to 220 BPM! Not only could I see it on the screen, I felt it in my chest. I immediately yelled to the doctor—he had his back turned and was talking with the nurse. 'GET ME OFF OF THIS THING", I shouted. He grabbed my arm, hit some buttons and started shouting instructions to his staff. "Get a crash cart, I need such and such IV started, just lotsa medical-ese. This was a scene right out of ER.

They laid me on a gurney that was in the room. I was still hooked up and lying there I could look backwards and upside down and see that my heart was still racing at 220 BPM. A nurse was busy prepping me with an IV line. I looked the doctor in the eye and demanded "What's going on? Am I in danger?" He turned away and didn't answer. Great.

This went on for several minutes—it felt like much longer. I was scared, but not to death. I was more pissed off!

DID I REALLY HAVE TO EXPERIENCE EVERY FREAKING THING THAT COULD POSSIBLY GO WRONG WITH THIS 33 YEARS OF FREAKING HEART BULLSHIT! I'd had enough!

As I lay there, just as suddenly as my heart rate spiked, it dropped to about 180 and started a steady reduction. I alerted the doctor, and just as the gal was ready to inject me with whatever they had lined up, he told her to wait. We all watched and within about 15 minutes I was in the 90 BPM range.

I asked the doc what had happened and he mumbled some sort of answer—whatever he said I didn't get or understand.

The important thing was that I had survived so that—all together now— I could go and "have another surgery!" (I've been getting way too much mileage out of that line . . .)

These heart healthy diets are just a little bit too extreme . . .

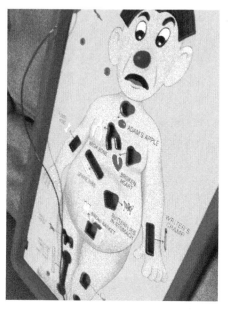

Practicing my surgical skillz—in case this guy doesn't work out. OK, Bob—suture self!

Healthy Heart Tip: Dudes–look straight down . . . if your moobs and gut obscure Mr. Happy then you'll likely have a 4 to 5 day stay in the ICU coming up real soon!

". . . Why can't Dr. Elkins live in Hawaii or Acapulco . . . anyplace but Oklahoma."

DR. ELKINS, MEET
DR. ELKINS!
20

Schedule yet another open heart surgery. Should be a piece of cake since I'd already done several times before, right? Well, actually—it was . . . once I came up with my brilliant idea.

Even though emotion plays a huge part in something like surgery, I took the approach of logic and common sense. Imagine! Since there was now the internet I would simply do some googling and find the top heart surgeons in the country and start from there.

I had had a follow up visit with Dr. Ward after my TEE. As per the usual, I asked him what he would do—did he have a preferred doctor that he recommended locally? I'm flat broke and travel costs would be difficult if not impossible.

Dr. Ward replied that he often recommended a local surgeon: Dr. Gravy was one of them. Dr. Gravy? Uhhhmmm . . . I'm the last person to judge someone based on names, however . . . Dr. Gravy? I later looked him up—the name is spelled Graeve, however, it's pronounced like something that you put on your spuds and clogs arteries. The good doctor's

129

other misfortune is that at first glance his name looks like a place where you put a coffin. Unfortunate.

I then asked Dr. Ward the question that shaped my decision: "Given that this will be my fourth time and given the extra complications that will factor in, if I could go to a top-ranked surgeon, would you recommend doing so over using Dr. Gravy?"

Dr. Ward's answer was a quick and simple yes.

I got my Google on and found phone numbers for 3 or 4 rock star surgeons to start with. I placed calls to each of them and at best got through office staff and of course, the first question was always "Who is your provider?" Some things never change, do they.

As I started this process I had a quick epiphany— perhaps even divinely inspired—it's funny that although God acts in mysterious ways he usually doesn't tell you how He did it.

Why don't I contact Dr. Elkins in Oklahoma City I thought— even though I'd heard that he wasn't practicing any more, he might have a recommendation! Am I good or what!!!!

I still had his email address and so I composed a brief description of my circumstance and fired it off. Are you sitting down? Good.

I received a response from Dr. Elkins within minutes. Let me repeat—within minutes! He wrote that yes, he remembered me and that he recommended the following course of action: His son would perform the surgery and he would assist. Two Elkins' for the price of one! I instantly conjured up images of having both Ken Griffey Sr. & Jr. in my lineup—and history showed that the kid was better than pops—perfect!

Theology 101: This would be an obvious example of divine intervention. I wouldn't need to think about it, discuss it pray over it, nosireebob! Elkins squared was the formula I was going with.

Of course, I shared this with my brothers and folks and they all readily agreed. The one downside would be that I'd have to go to Oklahoma City for the surgery and the week or so stay until my followup. I didn't have a dime.

This next part is frustrating, painful and not easy to tell.

During this time, especially when I had started to feel that things weren't right physically, I had shared my concerns with my brother Pete. I quite frankly told him that if it was indeed determined that I would need to have another surgery, that I would have to give it some thought—that I might just say screw it—I'm done.

What? . . . he started . . .

Look, Pete, I interjected— I'm broke, I couldn't afford a HappyMeal™ let alone the $5,000 deductible and besides, I've got nothing to look forward to.

ALERT: ANY surgery like this requires a certain state of mind —all systems have to be go. Besides, I continued, the last time was tricky enough for the surgeons—a normally fairly routine procedure is probably now a difficult undertaking; truth be told, I don't see the point. Maybe it's just my time to go.

Well, he got in my face and told me that I wasn't a quitter and that I was a fighter and so on and so forth.

I appreciated the support, but it wasn't him going thru this —it was me and I wasn't terribly interested in his two cents worth. Wanna know the ONLY reason why I ended up agreeing to go through with this?

My folks. We'd already lost our sister back in 2004 and they'd also gone through all of my health nonsense. I didn't want my parents to experience the stress and pain of maybe outliving another child.

But when I looked at it a little more objectively I realized that if I didn't have the operation, I could possibly still live another year or two as long as I wasn't active. If I had the surgery, yes, I could die, but the hope would be that I lived.

Another thing Pete said was that he'd have a discussion with our brother John and their wives—which they did, and they offered to cover my $5,000 deductible. Wow—thank you, guys. I was touched and moved and very grateful. Maybe this was gonna work out—everything was falling into place very smoothly.

The good news kept coming: When my dad and I had checked in early that morning for my TEE the previous week, the gal at the reception desk of the hospital mentioned that they had financial aid there. Financial aid? This wasn't none of that whacky Obama-care was it? (I'm a fiscal conservative and social moderate with left leanings and yes, I voted for Obama) . . . tell me more!

She did—and I filled out the application and gave it to her. You should know whether you qualify in a week or two—you'll be notified by mail she explained.

Well, I received notification that I DID qualify. Thank you Obamacare! What? It hadn't passed yet? Oh . . . my bad . . .

Here's where it gets really fun. The TEE cost . . . get this . . . $6,248—for a simple 45 minute procedure. Wow. However, with a $5,000 deductible and financial aid co-pay I just qualified for, they covered $4,200 of the tab—leaving ME, er, my brothers only $800 or so to cover. Man, I was so excited to tell them the good news! What a blessing! And they were obviously happy to hear it as well!

A few months later after the surgery, in March, I had received all the bills and the balance left on the deductible was around $800. I emailed both my brothers that information, as we had agreed to before the surgery. They both emailed back with "we'll have to discuss this with our wives."

I see.

I emailed back telling them not to bother—that I didn't need their money and would cover it myself. I ended up borrowing it from my folks.

That's the last time I've been in touch with them.

What if I hadn't received the financial aid? They had committed to covering $5,000 and now they renege on $800?

*I reached out to them in November of 2012 and we, along with their wives met for coffee. The details aren't important—what was important, especially to my parents who were greatly stressed over our estrangement, was that there was reconciliation. And so we chatted for a couple of hours. We didn't see eye to eye on everything—and that's ok—but we did part ways with the air cleared and a clean slate.

I continued with my preparations: the date had been set for December 15, 2011. If that seems a little bit quick— even though I needed the surgery, it wasn't emergent as in having had a heart attack—well the main reason was to get it done before my deductible restarted on January 1, 2012. Insurance games—fun for the entire family!

My brother John is a captain for Alaska Airlines and therefore had access to all sorts of travel connections and passes and points and who knows what else. he offered to make those arrangements for my folks and I.

John hooked us up with flights and a room at the Sheraton, which I would enjoy only if I survived the operation. I flew out on the 12th, having to stop through Vegas and then arriving in Oklahoma City on the 13th. I had to check in at the hospital for some tests, including my fourth cardio-cath, you know, the procedure where the anaphylactic shock had almost gotten me back in 1994! Not this time, baby!

My complete state of mind, soul, spirit—everything this time around was one of peace, calm, acceptance and complete faith in God.

Whatever happened, happened.

Where it was all about to happen-the view of the hospital from my hotel room the night before. Oklahoma in winter is a bleak place.

Healthy Heart Fact: Unfortunately, with four surgeries you DON'T get egg roll . . .

. . . "Let's Rock!" . . .—Al Bundy

A *CHIP* OFF THE OL' *BLOCK* 21

You'd think that whenever you do something **repeatedly** it would become **routine**, almost second nature. Isn't that what practice and repetition is all about? Heart surgery? Not so much.

I walked across the street from my hotel to the hospital—it was 7 am. I checked in with the folks that would be performing my cardio-cath. Since I had had the anaphylactic shock episode back in 1994, they would need to pre-medicate me with benadryl, amongst other meds.

I was led to my cubicle and changed into my gown. They did the usual prep-started some IV lines and such. It's funny—when the whole heart surgery thing impacted my life in 1979 my biggest concern was needles and shots. EVERYBODY hates needles and shots, right?

Now? I didn't even give it another thought. I'd look as they drew blood or ran a line or whatever—truth be told, the nurses and techs by and large did a great job. I snapped a few shots and provided some play by play on facebook!

I just laid there and waited. I was calm and relaxed. At a certain point a nurse came and said that it was almost time and that she would be administering the benadryl. OK—fine.

Within seconds I was trembling and higher than a kite—and continued feeling that way as they wheeled me into this incredibly cold and sterile/stainless steel looking . . . spaceship. I'm not kidding—this was unlike any other operating room I had ever seen.

They flopped/rolled me onto the . . . slab. OK—it wasn't a slab but it was really narrow and just different than what I had experienced before. There were 4/5 people in there —we chatted a little bit and . . . that's all I would remember.

Maybe one of these days I'll go to Oklahoma just to visit . . . nah . . .

I woke up in a hospital room. I would actually be spending the night in the hospital—my surgery was first thing in the morning, and this would be much more convenient. And, at approximately $10,000 per night, a real bargain!

That afternoon there was a knock on my door and in walked a man and woman—the man was wearing a white lab coat and I instantly knew he was Dr. Elkins. Junior. This was the first time that I had met him. Hopefully I'd see him again in about 24 hours.

He shook my hand and introduced his assistant Betsy. Dr. Elkins of course, resembled his father and had that one ingredient that was absolutely vital for every heart surgeon to have: Swag—he had major swagger. He made Mick Jagger look like the kid who got his ass kicked in one of those karate movies.

You'd **better** be a rock star if you're gonna saw someone's chest open, take their heart out or apart, repair it and put it back in/together—oh, all whilst keeping them alive!

In typical fashion he cut (that's a surgeon joke–come on!) right to the chase. "I looked at the TEE results, the treadmill and this morning's cath—I'm not gonna lie to you—this is gonna be an extremely difficult procedure and I put your survival at about 80–85%", he said.

Oh.

He then continued—we'll try to repair your valve first, because I'm not sure we'll be able to replace it. For one thing, we might not be able to cannulate you through your aorta for bypass and we might have to go through your femoral artery (which is what they ended up having to do), now, a repair won't last more than a few years, but doing a replacement will be much more dangerous. I believe that he then asked if I had a preference.

What?

I was not prepared to hear any of this. I answered, although not immediately, and I think I told him that I trusted him and that he should do whatever he felt was best.

This was, as always, in God's hands. We are taught to pray simply: Thy will be done. I added a little to it, however—in this case "Lord, I pray that YOUR will is that I survive this sucker!" It doesn't get any simpler does it?

They got up, we shook hands and that was that!

Wow.

I had a little bit of digesting to do, and I'm not referring to my yummy hospital lunch.

Later that evening my folks and my brother stopped by-they had just flown in and even though my brother would only stay until after my surgery the next day, my folks would be there for the duration. Them and me, in a single hotel room. More on that in the next chapter— see? I gave away the ending! I'm gonna survive this puppy!

Anyway, I shared what Dr. Elkins had said —

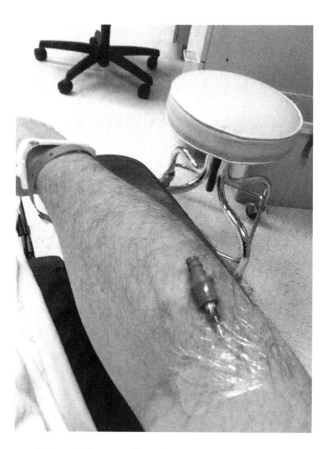

It's not the needles that get to me—it's the excruciating pain of the tape being pulled off!

it was a sobering few minutes, and then we said our goodbyes. I assured them that it would be a piece of cake and that I'd see them tomorrow afternoon.

I spent the rest of the evening channel surfing and playing around on my computer. This time, there would be no 4th annual "Last Supper" and Robert J. Newton stayed put in Salem. I certainly couldn't blame him!

And, as always, I slept like a baby.

> Hey Bud,
>
> Please let me know if there is anything we can do. Although its hard to believe now – Everything Does Happen for a Reason! You're in our thoughts & prayers.
>
> ✗–
>
> P.S. I don't have any of these "cool Commuters workout" post cards so I had to use one of these. Keep smiling (unless you want to cry--then cry!)

A thoughtful note from a longtime friend . . .

 The Business of Medicine Fact: The last major disease that a cure was discovered for was Polio—cures are NOT PROFITABLE. Treating symptoms of disease is. Do not be fooled—just follow the money.

"...Thank you, Lord—now; about your plan for the rest of my life . . ."

NOW WHAT? 22

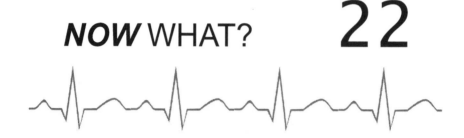

I was slowly starting to regain my senses. After the harrowing experience with the Shish-ka-BOB, . . . this is what is known as a running gag; a literary device used to display just how clever and witty I am!

When you first come out of anesthesia you are NOT coherent. Yes, you can hear voices and see things but at least for me, it's completely unfocused—but, enough about the 1970's. The nurse(s) ask you things and you react. I think. Or they'll tell you what they're gonna do and you agree. I think.

Now, your family, who they let in once you're "situated" say things like "you did great!" or, "you look great!" or—my favorite: "Hi, how are you feeling?"

As I've mentioned before, they give you a medicine called Versed which acts as an amnesiac. I'm just guessing but I think it's done in part because the whole process is somewhat traumatic and stressful. Heck, I sometimes feel like taking a little hit of it every time I watch Two and a Half Men.

EVERY surgery I've had results with my getting nauseous as I gain my bearings—it's the dry heaves because I hadn't anything to eat or drink in almost 24 hours, but it still sucks. Your gut hurts, your eyes water—it's like going through cold-turkey withdrawals, I've heard.

I did my heaving session and became aware that I had a tube down my throat and that my hands were tied to the rails of the bed because of it. Your natural instinct is to rip the tube out, and of course, it's there for a reason. I can't be sure, but it was removed fairly soon afterwards. The nurse preps you with instructions to breath and push and on the count of three they pull it out—even on the morphine it's extremely uncomfortable!

But hey—I'd cheated death yet one more time! I HAD to be way over my lifetime allotment by this time, right?

I would drift in and out of sleep/consciousness and either that evening or early the next morning I was taken out of the CCU and taken back to my room. My folks came by around 9 am or so—they were surprised cuz I was sitting in a chair next to the bed. I'd already had my breakfast—yoghurt, cereal, banana, juice, coffee—hey, where were my biscuits and gravy? Hmmm . . .

I can always sense the feeling of relief from my folks when I survive these surgeries. They gave me a replay of the previous day. Apparently about one hour into the surgery Dr. Elkins had come out to the waiting room and told my folks that he had not been able to repair the valve and that he would be replacing it. Even though I obviously had zero input at that time, it had been my preference to do a replacement—the last thing I wanted was yet another surgery a few years down the road—it was now or never.

The surgery had ended up taking 6 hours. I later found out that indeed I was placed on bypass through my groin instead of my heart. The scar there was about three inches long and took quite awhile longer than my chest incision to heal.

Speaking of scars, since this was my fourth surgery, each time they went in they would excise the old scar tissue—which in effect acted like getting a "vertical boob job!". As a result, I'm proud to report that I am now a perky B cup!

The next few days would be business as usual. Sleep, eat, watch TV, visit with my folks, get stuck for blood work every few hours, play around with my computer and post my usual nonsense on facebook—I'd actually done a 'streaming" running play by play using my iPhone and posting pics from wherever I could. It was almost like being there . . . not!

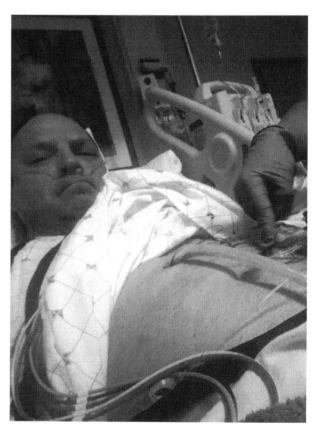

Removing one of my chest tubes. Truthfully not a major deal.

Right on schedule on the second day the nurse came to remove my Foley catheter. Not so fast there, Nurse Ratched! I explained my previous THREE episodes of catheter removal and the subsequent Shish–ka–BOB, and I wasn't willing to go through it again.

I told her that it was fine right where it was, thank you. In fact, maybe I'll leave it in just in case I need another surgery down the line . . .

Surprisingly she said OK—your choice.

Here's the deal—with my ADD—actually, I think I only have AD— and need to keep moving, I'd wanna get out and go for walks and use the bathroom instead of the bedpan as soon as possible. With that comes a whole orchestrated ordeal of organizing all the tubes and such.

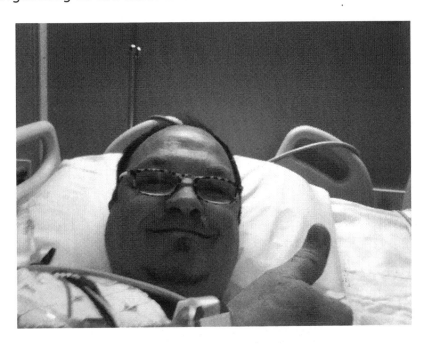

I had my IV lines. My Foley cath. My oxygen tube in my nostrils. My telemetry (wireless) heart monitor. Getting in and out of bed—by the way, you have to learn how to without using your arms due to the ZERO weight/stress you can put on your chest as your sternum heals—folks, you almost need a choreographer, director and producer! Or nurses—that's right, plenty of nurses.

Well, after another day or so I relented and out came the Foley. And within minutes I was peeing my brains out. I cried with sheer joy and happiness! Thank you, Lord!

On Saturday morning, the third day, my folks and I were chatting when there came a knock on the door. In walked a distinguished looking gentleman. It was Dr. Elkins senior! I was so excited and happy to see him. He was fit and trim and had to be 75 years old. He told us that it was a very difficult surgery and that it had been an honor and privilege for both him and his son to perform the operation. After a few minutes we said our goodbyes. It was an emotional event for me and I could tell that my folks were very moved as well.

On day five, it was time to check out. I got dressed, the nurse came by with my meds and instructions and I was wheeled to the lobby where my dad pulled up the rental car and, bundled up to brace against the cold midwest winter, we headed to the downtown Sheraton hotel.

I'll keep the next five days simple—the three of us shared a room with two Queen-sized beds. I could go off and nit pick, but the bottom line is that I was plenty comfortable. I will say that I heard sounds emanating from their bed that I had never heard before.

Old age—another thing to look forward to and deal with! Remember, we are all dying to live and living to die.

It was Christmas time, the decorations were up and the town was in a festive mood because the NBA's Thunder was about to start their season. The arena was just a block from the hotel and a day or two later I walked over. It was good to get out.

I've got to say this—I've read and heard about other's heart surgery recoveries—and even as experienced as I got, my

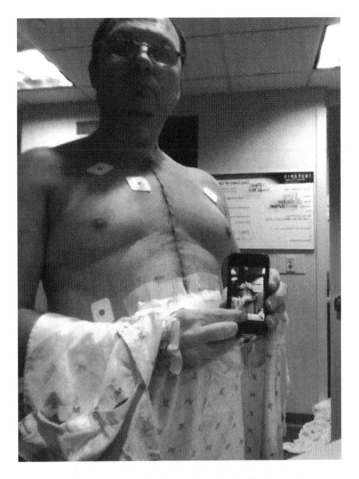

In all modesty, I can rock anybody in the heart surgery recovery/mobility department! . . . a skill I can do without! Getting ready to do another facebook post.

capacity for activity; walking, etc etc within DAYS of the operation, going back to work in a college classroom within two weeks is off the charts stunning and mind-boggling. The norm is two to three months to get into the swing of things.

I don't know the reason, but I've always been an energy guy —I walk with a stride and purpose . . . but I still am able to enjoy the flowers along the way. I believe that this ability has allowed me to persevere through all of this and is the motor to drive wherever this book and life takes me.

We flew back to Seattle on Christmas day. As we switched planes in Salt Lake City, there were three seats available—two in coach and one in first class. I turned left and found my seat— right next to my longtime friend Larry who was returning from seeing Stacey & Elliott in Santa Fe. What are the odds of that! With me, expect long odds!

Larry and I rockin' the First Class! More champagne, please . . . oh, and bring me a bag of those lovely peanuts, too!

What would a heart story be without the
obligatory "hugging your heart pillow" photo?

I'd like to say that we spent the next two hours chatting and sipping wine and celebrating my new lease. Remember, Larry had had his own heart surgery back in 1999. However, we didn't say a word to each other.

On the day after my surgery I tried to greet my folks as they came for their daily visit. I opened my mouth and NOTHING! I had lost my voice—it was attributed to that darn tube they had stuck down there. It happens now and then and time would be the only healer.

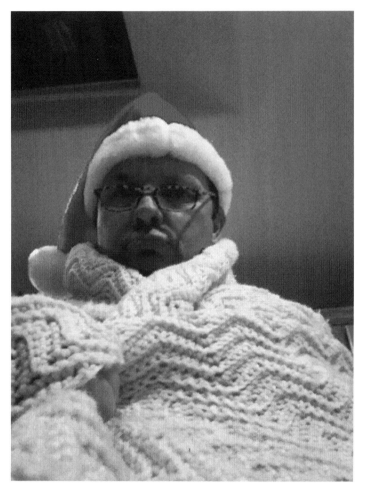

The Christmas Grinch! Brrr . . . SantaBob is freezing!

In fact, it was the toughest part of the five days in a cramped room with my folks. It wasn't that I didn't want to talk or that I was anti-social, I simply couldn't say a word!

We went to the store and bought throat lozenges and such, but it didn't help. I felt bad, cuz I know it appeared that I was being sullen—but I wasn't! I was truly happy to still be here!

So I sit down next to Larry—he lights up with a big smile and

I could only shrug my shoulders.

Here's what I did. I busted out my computer and would answer his questions in my notepad program. It wasn't ideal but it worked well enough.

We arrived in Seattle and got home around 9 pm. Having been gone for almost two weeks, their house was freezing! Literally! We warmed up and got ready for bed.

Whew—another wild ride. Over. Or was it? I was still taking percocets and other meds—the pain, although not debilitating, is still pronounced enough to need help with.

A few days later I had an adverse reaction to one of the meds—I plumped up like a Ball Park Frank and had a burning rash all over my body. I contacted OKC and they told me to stop taking it and within a day or two things were back to normal.

For the next month or so I took it easy enough. I'd go for walks, take naps, spend time on my computer and explore opportunities for making money. If it weren't for my folks and not only their hospitality but their financial assistance in lending me monies for my bills I couldn't have done this. I truly would've been out on the street. Imagine recovering from open heart surgery during the winter, homeless on the streets of the Northwest.

Thanks again, mom & dad!

I was able to start driving within a couple of weeks. Independence is HUGE in any recovery. It just is.

By February I was feeling pretty darn good. And, once again, I had to reinvent myself. But how? Where? What?

My congenital aortic stenosis, first diagnosed in January of 1979 had now consumed 33 years—pretty much my entire adult life. And it and it's effect will never be gone.

It has compromised my ability to live fully and without restrictions.

It has impacted my emotional state.

It eliminated my ability to make a living of my choosing.

It has devastated my capacity for maximizing my love of sports.

Nothing, in life, of and by itself should take away our desire to survive. It's in our nature—an instinct, yet, I'm also aware of and sensitive to those that succumb, for whatever reason. Furthermore, the cumulative effect of many challenges on all fronts can wear one down.

What's that? Oh yeah—we call that an ASS-KICKING! I've been in that position and it's, well, sorta like getting your ass kicked . . . I digress . . .

At some point, you quit fighting it. It's acceptance. It's letting go—and letting God, as the saying goes.

God has been there for the big events . . . now, I desperately need a few of His bones and breadcrumbs.

Even so, I still retained my spirit, fight and resolve to not only continue to deal with it but I'm more determined than ever to give meaning and respect to my experience in any way that will benefit others.

What does that look like?

I have no idea.

Maybe this book is a start.

Healthy Heart Hint: If you have a dog, think of the dog as an exercise machine with fur. A brisk walk with the dog is good for both of your hearts.

". . . It's true—I walk on water. Ok; so it's frozen . . . but that doesn't change the fact that it's water . . . "

THE *MESSIAH* COMPLEX   23

"Bob, you have a Messiah Complex."

That was the **verdict** by my **longtime pastor** and friend Dale.

We were having lunch in Enumclaw, Washington. It was Tuesday, October 30, 2012. I'd known Dale for over 20 years— his son Brad was a student of mine back in '92. I'd videotaped his other son Jeff's wedding and I occasionally played bass for his church's worship band. We would get together to drink lots of coffee and solve the world's problems.

I had driven up from Clearlake, CA., where I had been staying with my longtime friends Mike & Madlyn, to see my cardiologist. Even though I'm supposed to see him twice a year, I hadn't been since my surgery the previous December—with the exception of the initial follow up, which was around the middle of January.

I was once again experiencing symptoms.

Good Lord.

Fatigue, shortness of breath and lack of stamina. When I tried exercising I just couldn't get it going. It wasn't gasping, sucking for air—just an inability to increase my heart rate and work up a sweat. I suspected—anything other than needing yet another surgery— that the culprit was a medication I was on called Metoprolol. I took it twice a day; basically it's a beta blocker and it was to control my heart rate/blood pressure and help stabilize my heart's "electronics." For years I've had an irregular heartbeat and the Metoprolol straightened all that out!

Of course, like all good drugs, using it could result in an annoying side effect or hundred—check these out—some of which I seemed to be experiencing.

"According to studies, about 27% of patients who use Metoprolol experience at least one side effect. Some of them are mild and transient but can be quite serious and require urgent medical attention. Metoprolol can be metabolized in two ways and patients who are slow metabolizers may experience severe side effects more often. Most common side effects of Metoprolol:

- *Headache*
- *Tiredness*
- *Dizziness*
- *Tinnitus (ringing in one or both ears)*
- *Drowsiness*
- *Anxiety*
- *Confusion*
- *Lightheadedness*
- *Foggy thinking*
- *Fainting spells*
- *Ataxia*
- *Short-term memory loss*
- *Cold, tingling, or numbness in fingers and toes*
- *Arthralgias*

- *Muscle pain*
- *Cramps*
- *Mild flu symptoms (chills, fever, runny nose, cough and sore throat)*
- *Increased asthma attacks in patients with pre-existing asthma*
- *Shortness of breath*
- *Wheezing*
- *Low blood pressure*
- *Chest pain*
- *Slow heart rate*
- *Arrhythmia*
- *Difficulty in swallowing*
- *Increased thirst*
- *Dry mouth*
- *Nausea*
- *Vomiting*
- *Heartburn*
- *Stomach pain*
- *Constipation*
- *Gas*
- *Diarrhea*
- *Decreased urination*
- *Reversible hair loss (alopecia)*
- *Dry mouth or eyes*
- *Conjunctivitis*
- *Eye pain*
- *Decreased vision clearness*
- *Yellowing of the skin or eyes*
- *Swelling and redness at injection site*
- *Itching*
- *Urticaria*
- *Unexplained rash*
- *Somnolence*
- *Insomnia*

- *Nightmares*
- *Depression*
- *Sexual dysfunction*
- *Erectile dysfunction*
- *Peyronie's disease*

Want more? Other less common side effects of Metoprolol:

- *Hepatitis*
- *Worsening of psoriasis*
- *Photosensitivity*
- *Arthritis*
- *Claudication*
- *Anorexia*
- *Diabetes mellitus*
- *Red, swollen, blistered, or peeling skin*
- *Generalized psoriasiform lesions*
- *Arterial insufficiency of the Raynaud type*
- *Palpitations*
- *Emotional lability*
- *Slightly clouded sensorium*
- *Paresthesias*
- *Retroperitoneal fibrosis*

"Sudden discontinuation of the use of Metoprolol can also cause side effects. It can cause such adverse reactions as sweating, chest pain, breathing difficulty and arrhythmia (irregular or fast heartbeat). In patients suffering from angina pectoris, discontinuation of Metoprolol intake can cause very serious aggravation of the angina symptoms. Like any other medicine, Metoprolol can cause allergic reactions that can manifest as:

- *Severe dizziness*

- *Unexplained rash*
- *Hives*
- *Itching*
- *Unexplained swelling of the face, eyes, mouth, lips, tongue, neck*
- *Wheezing*
- *Unusual hoarseness*
- *Difficulty in breathing or swallowing*
- *Tightness in the chest*

Now, for the **serious** side effects!

- *Unexplained swelling the arms, legs, hands, or feet (peripheral edema)*
- *Sudden weight gain*
- *Hypotension*
- *Arrhythmia (severe bradycardia or irregular heartbeat)*
- *Heart block of the first-, second- or third-degree*
- *Intensification of AV block*
- *Variant angina pectoris (coronary artery spasm)*
- *Congestive heart failure*
- *Cardiogenic shock (especially when used post myocardial infarction)*
- *Increased bronchospasm*
- *Severe respiratory distress*
- *Severe dizziness or lightheadedness*
- *Hepatitis*
- *Bowel or urethral obstruction*
- *Hypoglycemia*
- *Hyponatriemia (confusion, seizures, sluggishness)*
- *Hyperkalemia*
- *Unusual bruising or bleeding*
- *Hallucinations*
- *Disorientation for time and place*
- *Mental depression up to catatonia*

- *Polymyalgia rheumatica*
- *Gangrene*

Metoprolol can also cause aggravation of breathing difficulties in patients with obstructive lung diseases such as asthma, chronic bronchitis, or emphysema.

But at least my heart rate was under control!!!!!

I had called and scheduled my appointment for that coming Friday, the 2nd of November. Wanna know my deep down gut feeling? I could almost care less and at the same time I was more angry, frustrated and disappointed than ever. How could I not be?

However—if the doctor even HINTED at needing another surgery . . . I was done—I'll see you on the other side.

Or not.

And so, as Dale and I engaged in our conversation I expressed my feelings to him. I also told him that I was not satisfied with just surviving my surgeries and being alive and taking up space. There's existing and there's living. Existing is not enough. Sounds like the title of a James Bond flick, doesn't it? And, I wanted to live.

I continued with "although I didn't enjoy these past 33 years of health challenges, I am here and I've had an amazing experience that God allowed not only to happen but also likely had a hand in me surviving. It would make me feel like there was some value and meaning to it all if I could somehow use this unprecedented experience to help others. Cuz otherwise, it all feels like a big waste."

"Bob, you have a Messiah Complex."

My initial reaction was one of ..."no, I don't—and you're full of shit." Truth be told, I didn't even know what a Messiah Complex was, but I could venture a pretty good guess—and it wasn't flattering. But, I continued listening to him.

All I wanted was some peace. A home of my own—it had been over 8 years since I had slept in my own bed—I didn't even OWN a bed anymore. Gainful employment instead of a hand to mouth existence. A sense of belonging and being a part of something. Community. Companionship. Doesn't sound like a Messiah Complex to me—I wasn't out to change the world.

Later that day I Googled Messiah Complex. Here's what Wikipedia has to say about it:

A messiah complex (also known as the Christ complex or savior complex) is a state of mind in which an individual holds a belief they are, or are destined to become, a savior. The messiah complex does not appear in the Diagnostic and Statistical Manual of Mental Disorders.

Oh good—at least I'm not a nutjob.

For the majority of the 33 years and counting journey of heart escapades I have had a pretty clear and consistent position on God's role/participation in my ongoing adventure.

I'll keep this real simple.

I believe that God is sovereign and can do what He wants. And, as a sovereign God he owes me only his wrath and fury, yet He gives me his grace and mercy.

I believe that Jesus is my savior and I accepted him at age

13. I have also since committed more sins than just might be humanly possible—and when I do, I'm almost always reminded by that little angel/guilt dude sitting on my shoulder.

As I said earlier, I keep my prayers as simple as "Your will be done". Does God answer prayer? I'm sure He does.

Has God predestined every thing I do, say, think, feel? Nope. And, if He DID, then nothing is my fault!

Does God know everything that's gonna happen? That's a tricky one and I have a long and complicated opinion on that, which I will address in my next book tentatively entitled "*I Know Nuthink*", which will be dedicated to Sgt. Schultz of Hogan's Hero's fame . . .

Do I hold ANYBODY that opens up their pie-hole with ANY proclamation about God/Jesus to a higher standard? Yes!!

The second someone says that "they've been called to do "xyz", my ears perk up. I am now looking to bust them. This comes from many experiences with people doing dubious things in the name of Jesus. I do lots of dubious things, too. And the very best thing I can do is to SHUT MY MOUTH and try to get it right with my actions.

I would love for God to orchestrate a career for the remainder of my life that allows for me to make a living and give back. I promise this: I don't know what that looks like, but I DO know that for it to happen I'd better get busy.

After all—it might be part of God's plan!

I went to see Dr. Ward on November 2nd, and after an echo-ultrasound, blood work and rudimentary exam, Dr. Ward, based on my complaints and symptoms, prescribed that I go OFF the Metoprolol. Goodbye side effects/symptoms, hello irregular heartbeat . . . everything has it's price . . . right?

And Dale? Still a valued friend and confidant.

The Messiah Complex?

Don't we all have a little bit of that in us? The desire to make a difference? To give back. To make sense of all that we live and experience?

That's all I want. I know that God knows my heart—no pun intended—and that He's smiling down on me. And . . . He's smiling down on you, too.

Even though this is the end of my book, my story will never be over—it will end when I do. And so in the meantime I'm gonna do my best to make the best of this adventure—and enjoy doing so.

That's all we can do. That's what you'll do, too when faced with the same.

And, as Dale always says . . . Shalom.

Peace.

My FINAL Healthy Heart Tip: Even tho' I enjoyed telling my story and making it readable, open heart surgery is a BITCH! It's also largely avoidable. I didn't have a choice—YOU DO!

ACKNOWLEDGMENTS

Thank-you's serve two purposes as far as I'm concerned: to give praise for a job well done and to identify those we can blame in case we suck.

I could easily list hundreds of people when it comes to thanking them for their prayers, love and support during my health problems. You know who you are and, once again, thank you!

And so, I'd like to limit these thank you's to those directly involved in the writing of this book.

I'll start with my life-long friend Robert J. Newton. Robert (don't call me Bob) actually challenged me to tell my story in November of 1999. We were having breakfast, and I got on my soap-box about his grease-laden unhealthy selection—he replied with " If you're really that passionate about people's health, I want you to record an audio book on CD about your experiences, no holds barred, and have it to me by January 15th". Not being one to turn down a challenge, I dug right in, and the original "*Straight From My Heart*" was born—an 80-minute audio book about my experiences dealing with (at the time) three open heart surgeries.

I initially duplicated several dozen copies and sent them out to family and friends—I wanted their feedback, but maybe even more importantly, I wanted them to hear how I truly felt about what I had experienced.

The response was overwhelming. Yeah, a few people got their feathers ruffled—the truth can be painful, especially for those who are reliving events whilst writing about them —but almost everyone encouraged me to continue my mission of telling my story. And so I am. Thanks, Robert.

Of course I must thank my family—you've just read about them.

Joy, my ex-girlfriend (but still a best friend) also suggested (before Robert's challenge, as I recall) that I write a book—my stories kept coming and maybe she thought that it would be good therapy. She was right.

I'd also like to thank Yvonne. After encouraging me to get back on track (self motivation can be a bitch), I emailed rough drafts to her and she provided much needed and appreciated input as well as massive grammatical/spelling fixes. Even though we've drifted apart I enjoyed her contribution. Thanks!

And finally, my friend Dave, whom I've know since high school. Dave is a talented drummer and a quick wit—often at the same time—and we've worked together on occasion, including an incredible Hawaiian tour! I mentioned to him that I was compiling all of my stories and experiences into a book, and as a goof I emailed him a chapter. He emailed back changes—they really made a difference, making me appear much cooler than I am. And isn't that what editors and friends are truly for?

Since I know that I'll forget somebody, I want to apologize in advance and thank those whom I've forgotten to thank. But like the Oscars award show on TV, (where the orchestra starts playing hint music i.e., time to shut up) I think I can hear the violins starting to warm up . . .

ABOUT **THE AUTHOR** -*BOB SLUYS*

Bob Sluys is a recognized authority, from a patient's perspective, on open heart surgery-as he should be having survived four procedures. A native of The Netherlands, he spent his formative years in Seattle. In addition to his health challenges he also squeezed in several careers as well—over 30 years traveling the world as an entertainer, six years spent teaching college, a stint as a top-producing real estate agent and, he even built a website featuring his alter-ego . . . ScrabbleGuy! Bob currently play bass with The Beer Barrel Boyz and, can still beat anybody in a game of H.O.R.S.E. —except for possibly Michael Jordan.

Bob's passion is in helping others get their story out.

SO—WHAT'S *YOUR* STORY?

You've just read mine. But, what about *your* story? After all, we all have them and they're ALL unique—at least to ourselves. They're also special and need to not only be told but sometimes heard as well.

That's where I can come in.

Allow me to help you write YOUR story.

Sometimes when we have events in our lives—big or small, tragic or happy—it doesn't matter—processing them through journaling, recording, sharing verbally by groaning and moaning or praising and celebrating not only provides release and closure but a sense of accomplishment as well.

Truth be told, I cannot even begin to quantify the tremendous benefit I received from writing this book. Just the therapeutic value is off the charts—and WAY cheaper than a shrink, I promise you!

Just as you are holding my story in your hands right now, I

can help put your story in other peoples hands as well. Or, on their computer—I can even create audio books or videos, too.

I'm professional, competent, discreet and more importantly, sensitive to your needs because as you know—I've been there. In fact, I'm still there and probably always will be.

Please feel free to contact me for a free and confidential consultation. I'd love to hear what's on your mind and, in your heart.

Find me on facebook— http://www.facebook.com/bob.sluys

Please visit the *Straight From My Heart* facebook page as well: http://www.facebook.com/pages/Straight-From-My-Heart

Also by the author . . .

Memoirs Of A Nobody

—A collection of over 60 true-life short stories from the amazing adventure that is his life. Told in the same direct and humorous style as *Straight From My Heart*, you'll read about his career in show biz—from a harrowing escape from China, travels to an AIDS orphanage in South Africa—and everything in between. Can all of this have actually happened to somebody NOT named Hemingway . . . ?

Yes it has!